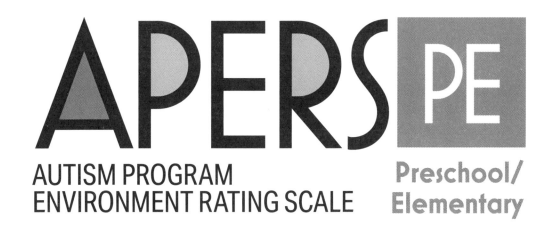

APERS PE

AUTISM PROGRAM ENVIRONMENT RATING SCALE

Preschool/ Elementary

User's Guide

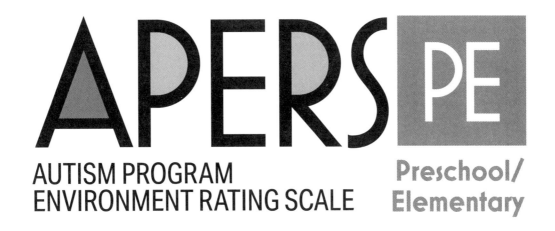

APERS PE

AUTISM PROGRAM ENVIRONMENT RATING SCALE

Preschool/ Elementary

User's Guide

by

Samuel L. Odom, Ph.D.

Ann M. Sam, Ph.D.

and

Ann W. Cox, Ph.D.

Frank Porter Graham Child Development Institute
University of North Carolina at Chapel Hill

·P A U L·H·
BROOKES
PUBLISHING CO.®

Baltimore • London • Sydney

Paul H. Brookes Publishing Co.
Post Office Box 10624
Baltimore, Maryland 21285-0624
USA

www.brookespublishing.com

Typeset by Progressive Publishing Services, York, Pennsylvania.
Manufactured in the United States of America by
Versa Press, Inc., East Peoria, Illinois.

APERS work was made possible by grants from multiple funding agencies. The Office of Special Education Programs funded the National Professional Development Center for Autism (Grant No. H325G070004), through which the APERS was originally developed. The middle/high school version of the APERS was developed through the Center on Secondary Education for Students with Autism Spectrum Disorder (Grant No. R324C120006), funded through the Institute of Education Sciences (IES). The preschool/elementary version of the APERS was further developed through the Efficacy Study of Elementary Learners with Autism (Grant No. R324A150047), also funded through IES. The opinions expressed herein, however, are those of the authors and do not represent views of the Institute or of the U.S. Department of Education.

For information on the components of the *Autism Program Environment Rating Scale–Preschool/Elementary (APERS-PE),* visit https://brookespublishing.com/product/apers/

Stock photo © iStockphoto.com.

Library of Congress Cataloging-in-Publication Data

Names: Odom, Samuel L., author. | Sam, Ann M., author. | Cox, Ann W., author.
Title: Autism Program Environment Rating Scale–Preschool/Elementary
    (APERS-PE) User's Guide / by Samuel L. Odom, Ann M. Sam, and Ann W. Cox.
Description: Baltimore, Maryland : Paul H. Brookes Publishing Co., [2023] | Includes
    bibliographical references and index.
Identifiers: LCCN 2022049842 | ISBN 9781681257242 (Paperback)
Subjects: LCSH: Children with autism spectrum disorders—Education (Elementary) |
    Educational evaluation—Methodology—Handbooks, manuals, etc.
Classification: LCC LC4717 .O46 2023 | DDC 371.94—dc23/eng/20221028
LC record available at https://lccn.loc.gov/2022049842

British Library Cataloguing in Publication data are available from the British Library.

2027   2026   2025   2024   2023

10   9   8   7   6   5   4   3   2   1

Contents

About the Downloads

Purchasers of this book may download, print, and/or photocopy the following materials for professional use.

For conducting a full APERS-PE evaluation:

- The Scoring Tool, provided as an Excel spreadsheet

  - **IMPORTANT NOTE ABOUT THE SCORING TOOL:** In order for the Scoring Tool to function correctly, macros must be enabled within the Excel file. See the "Instructions for Enabling Macros.pdf" for instructions on how to enable macros for this file.

- The Record Review Guide, Observer Guide, and interview protocols. The interview protocols are provided as fillable PDFs for note-taking purposes.

- Additional downloadable forms provided as chapter appendices.

For conducting the APERS-PE Self-Assessment only:

- The APERS-PE Self-Assessment Tool, provided as an Excel spreadsheet

  - **IMPORTANT NOTE ABOUT THE SELF-ASSESSMENT TOOL:** In order for the Self-Assessment Tool to function correctly, macros must be enabled within the Excel file. See the "Instructions for Enabling Macros.pdf" for instructions on how to enable macros for this file.

To access the materials that come with this book:

1. Go to the Brookes Publishing Download Hub: http://downloads.brookespublishing.com

2. Register to create an account (or log in with an existing account)

3. Redeem the code HWpHxPNng to access any locked materials.

About the Authors

Samuel L. Odom, Ph.D., Senior Research Scientist, Frank Porter Graham Child Development Institute, University of North Carolina at Chapel Hill

Dr. Odom is former Director of the Frank Porter Graham Child Development Institute (FPG), University of North Carolina at Chapel Hill, where he remains as Senior Research Scientist. At FPG, he co-directs the National Clearinghouse on Autism Evidence and Practice. In addition, he is an adjunct professor at San Diego State University. Dr. Odom is the author or coauthor of more than 200 journal articles and book chapters and has edited 10 books on early childhood intervention and developmental disabilities. His current research is addressing treatment efficacy for children and youth with autism, identification of evidence-based practices, and implementation science. In 2013, he received the Arnold Lucius Gesell Prize awarded for career achievement in research on social inclusion and child development from the Theodor Hellbrügge Foundation in Munich, Germany. In 2016, he received an honorary doctoral degree from Stockholm University.

Ann M. Sam, Ph.D., Senior Research Scientist, Frank Porter Graham Child Development Institute, University of North Carolina at Chapel Hill

Dr. Sam is Senior Research Scientist at the Frank Porter Graham Child Development Institute (FPG) at the University of North Carolina at Chapel Hill. Dr. Sam's research interests were shaped by her experiences as a public school teacher working with students with autism. The primary goal of her work is to increase awareness and use of evidence-based practices by educators and practitioners. Dr. Sam led the development of the Autism Focused Intervention Resources and Modules (AFIRM), which provide free, online modules related to evidence-based practices for children and youth with autism.

Ann W. Cox, MSN, Ph.D., Research Scientist (retired), Frank Porter Graham Child Development Institute, University of North Carolina at Chapel Hill

Dr. Cox's career has spanned some more than 40 years, emphasizing the development and implementation of programs for young and school-age children with disabilities and their families. She has addressed the need for current and future personnel to develop the skills necessary for implementing sound, research-based practices within an interdisciplinary environment. Prior to her retirement, Dr. Cox was Director of the National Professional Development Center on ASD and other related educational research programs at the Frank Porter Graham Child Development Institute at the University of North Carolina at Chapel Hill. As such, she was instrumental in developing, evaluating, and modifying the Autism Program Environment Rating Scale and other educational materials on evidence-based practices for students with autism.

Preface

The development of the Autism Program Environment Rating Scale (APERS) began in 2008. The adage that "necessity is the mother of invention" is very aptly applied to the development of the APERS. At the time, the National Professional Development Center on Autism (NPDC) had been funded with the mission to increase service providers' (i.e., primarily teachers') use of evidence-based practices for children and youth with autism. Such practices are situated within a program environment. Our experience in classrooms indicated that there was a large range of quality in such programs, but there was not yet a reliable or valid way of assessing program quality. A systematic assessment of program quality would specify features of programs that are important to the learning process, providing necessary information for program improvement. Thus, members of the NPDC took on the task of developing such an assessment. In the years since, this assessment has been further developed and refined and now exists in two versions: the Autism Program Environment Rating Scale–Preschool/Elementary (APERS-PE), described in this manual, and the Autism Program Environment Rating Scale–Middle/High School (APERS-MH), available separately. Additional information about the development of the APERS is provided in Chapter 1.

Acknowledgments

Since 2007, many talented colleagues have contributed their expertise to the development of the APERS. We were first inspired by the work of Ilene Schwartz and her colleagues with an earlier professional development center focusing on autism. Their initial efforts in working with individual programs created a path and direction for our subsequent work. We describe the APERS instrument development process in Chapter 1, but we do not acknowledge the many people that contributed to the ongoing development of the APERS. First, we want to acknowledge two initial program leaders, Deborah Hatton, now deceased, and Gail Houle, who was our first program officer at the Office of Special Education Programs. The list of contributors over the years is extensive, including Brian Boyd, Matt Brock, Leann DuWalt, Shayla Green, Laura Hall, Susan Hedges, Kara Hume, Bonnie Kraemer, Suzanne Kucharczyk, Becky Dees, Jennifer Neitzel, Yolanda Perkins, Stephanie Rezska, Sally Rogers, Evelyn Shaw, John Sideris, Jessica Steinbrenner, Kate Szidon, and John Thomas. Also, we are very appreciative of the time and tolerance of the many teachers, administrators, related service providers, and parents who have participated in interviews and allowed us to observe in their classrooms.

*In remembrance of Deborah Hatton, the first Director
of the National Professional Development Center on Autism
at the Frank Porter Graham Child Development Institute, University
of North Carolina at Chapel Hill. Her energy, dedication, and wisdom
paved the way for the development of the original versions of the APERS.*

1 Introduction to the Autism Program Environment Rating Scale

> Care and Quality are internal and external aspects of the same thing. A person who sees Quality and feels it as (s)he works is a person who cares. A person who cares about what (s)he sees and does is a person who's bound to have some characteristic of quality.
>
> —Robert M. Pirsig (1975)

If a child with autism enters the public school system at 3 years of age and graduates or leaves the system at age 22, they will have spent 19 years and as many as 1,200,000 minutes in school (19 years × 180 days × 6 hours × 60 minutes). Aside from home and family, this would make school programs the most influential settings for development and learning; in fact, the educational system has been called children's/youth's "best hope" for the future (Odom et al., 2014). This hope, however, is based on an assumption that children with autism will experience high-quality educational programs (i.e., ones that have a positive learning environment and appropriately organized classroom settings, effective educational techniques, involvement of and respect for families, and a collaborative professional team). The Autism Program Environment Rating Scale (APERS) is an assessment of the quality of educational programs for children and youth with autism. The information it provides can be used to improve the quality of educational programs for children and youth with autism. Two versions of the APERS are available: the APERS-PE for preschool and elementary programs and the APERS-MH for middle and high school programs. In this chapter, we briefly introduce our concept of program quality, provide an overview of the APERS-PE, describe efforts to assess program quality in other areas of education, chronicle the history of the APERS development, and describe the sections of this manual that document the procedural features of the APERS.

(*Note:* Throughout this manual, we use the term "autism" as well as both person-first and identity-first descriptors.)

THE APERS AND PROGRAM QUALITY

Program quality refers to how well or poorly features of a program accomplish the goal for which the program is intended. The goal of most educational programs for children with autism is to promote learning, development, and participation. The program provides the setting in which teachers, related services providers such as speech-language pathologists (SLPs), and paraprofessionals can employ evidence-based practices with fidelity. Program quality exists on a continuum from high quality, which reflect optimal excellence that one may expect in a program, to low quality, in which the program exhibits features that are unacceptable and may even have deleterious effects for children.

1

The APERS-PE was designed to measure the quality of preschool and elementary school programs based on the educational needs of most children with autism. It was created in response to an increased demand for special education services for children with autism, the need to evaluate the quality of those service provided, and the absence of a reliable and valid assessment to provide such evaluative information. The APERS-PE differs from other broader measures of general program quality, such as the Early Childhood Environmental Rating Scale–Third Edition. (ECERS; Harms, Clifford, & Cryer, 2014) or the Classroom Assessment Scoring System (CLASS; Laparo et al., 2004) because it focuses specifically on the unique learning needs of children with autism rather than general program environment.

APERS-PE AT A GLANCE

The following sections provide a brief overview of the APERS-PE: its purpose, limitations, and the overall structure of the assessment instrument; how and by whom the APERS is used; and the components included in the APERS-PE kit.

Purpose, Limitations, and Structure

The information from the APERS-PE, which is discussed in subsequent chapters, highlights the strengths and weakness in program quality of preschool and elementary school programs. It generates quantitative "scores" that reflect the continuum from poor to excellent total quality as well as a profile of specific features of programs and how quality may vary across the features. The APERS-PE is a program evaluation tool intended for use as a formative resource for improving learning and educational environments for students with autism and represents a "snapshot" of a program. Information gathered from the APERS should be used to identify aspects of excellent educational programs that support students with autism, as well as those that may need improvement/refinement.

The APERS-PE assessment instrument consists of 62 items organized within 10 domains: 1) Learning Environments, 2) Positive Learning Climate, 3) Assessment and Individualized Educational Program (IEP) Development, 4) Curriculum and Instruction, 5) Communication, 6) Social Competence, 7) Personal Independence and Competence, 8) Interfering Behavior, 9) Family Involvement, and 10) Teaming. These domains represent important aspects of program quality for students with autism.

Use of the APERS-PE

The APERS-PE was designed for use by practitioners interested in assessing the quality of programs for children with autism. These practitioners may be administrators, autism program supervisors, program evaluators, special education teachers, or related services professionals (e.g., SLPs, school psychologists). In addition, the APERS-PE may be used by researchers to answer specific research questions related to program quality. It may be administered in inclusive programs, self-contained programs, or programs that combine elements of both. Raters should plan on one full day to conduct the classroom observation portion of the APERS-PE and a second to review student records and interview program staff.

The APERS-PE examiners gather information about the program through 1) classroom observations, 2) interviews with school staff and family members, and 3) review of student records (particularly IEPs) for two or three students with autism. The examiner takes notes about their findings during each part of this information-gathering process. After completing this process, the examiner reviews the notes and completes the assessment items in the Scoring Tool based on the information gathered. To do so, the examiner checks off indicators for each item. Scoring the APERS-PE takes approximately 75 minutes. The Scoring Tool automatically generates the following:

- Item scores based on the indicators checked off for each item

- Overall program scores

- Scores for each domain (and dimensions within these domains)

- Graphs of these scores to provide a visual snapshot of program quality

The rater writes a report based on the results and shares feedback with the program staff.

APERS Kit Components

In addition to this manual, the APERS-PE kit includes the following components. Subsequent chapters discuss in greater depth about how to use each one to administer and score the APERS-PE:

- *Observer Guide:* One-page guide for the rater to keep on hand and refer to as needed during classroom observations

- *Records Review Guide:* One-page guide for the rater to keep on hand and refer to as needed while reviewing student records

- *Interview Protocols:* Six protocols for conducting a preliminary interview as well as interviews with a special educator, general educator, parent, administrator, and SLP. These protocols include interview guidelines and questions and space for recording responses.

- *Scoring Tool:* Excel spreadsheet for completing APERS-PE items and scoring the APERS-PE, as previously described

- *APERS-PE Self-Assessment (APERS-PE/SA) Tool:* The self-assessment is an optional self-rating scale, similar to the full APERS-PE assessment but shorter. It is specifically designed for teachers and other service providers to rate their own program to obtain information for their own internal use in program improvement.

In addition, this manual includes two appendices: Frequently Asked Questions and a Glossary of terms used within assessment items in the Scoring Tool.

The following sections discuss the APERS in the context of how quality is assessed in education and explain in greater detail why and how the APERS was developed.

CONTEXT FOR THE APERS: ASSESSMENT OF QUALITY IN EDUCATION

Assessment of quality in the field of education is an elusive endeavor. Although different entities such as professional associations, state governments, and even the federal government have established national standards or guidelines, they primarily identify the kinds of services that need to be in place but rarely "drill down" to aspects or features of programs that make them high or low quality (see Figure 1.1). The exceptions to this general state of the field are program quality assessment initiatives in early childhood education, after-school programs, and the emerging area of assessment of quality in programs for students with autism.

Program Quality in Early Childhood Education

The assessment of the quality of educational program environments has been the strongest in early childhood education. The initial early childhood assessment instruments focused on preschool child care settings, with authors adapting the assessments for other educational environments and assessments. The three assessments serving as the best examples are the Early Childhood Environmental Rating Scale (ECERS; Harms & Clifford, 1980), the CLASS (LaParo et al., 2004), and the Inclusive Classroom Profile (ICP; Soukakou, 2016).

ECERS: Focus on Classroom Quality The ECERS was developed because of a concern for the poor quality that was occurring in early childhood education and a need to improve it (R. M. Clifford, December 2011), Harms and Clifford (1980) developed a scale that employed a 7-point Likert-type format, with behavioral anchors for the 1 (lowest), 3, 5, and 7 rating points. To complete the ratings, the rater observes in a classroom for a day or more and gathers information

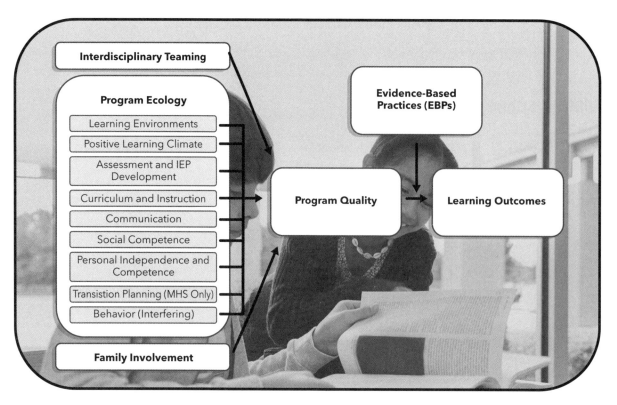

Figure 1.1.   Conceptual framework for the APERS.

from the teachers when necessary. The original ECERS focused on the structural quality of the class. Now in its third edition (Harms, Clifford, & Cryer, 2014), the current version of the scale has grouped 35 items into five domains (Space and Furnishings, Personal Care Routines, Language and Literacy, Learning Activities, and Program Structure), with thorough psychometric analyses to support this grouping. In addition to the ECERS, these authors have developed similar quality rating scales for infants and toddler programs (Harms et al., 2016), family child care settings (Harms et al., 2022), and school-age care settings (Harms et al., 2014). All the scales are now in their second or third editions and follow a systematic process for establishing acceptable psychometric features of the instruments.

CLASS: Focus on Teacher-Student Interactions   To accomplish a similar goal of assessing early childhood environments, Pianta and colleagues (LaParo et al., 2004) developed a rating scale called the CLASS, which focuses more on teacher–student interactions in preschool classes than the structural ecology of those settings, as assessed in the ECERS. Also, the system differs from the ECERS because raters generally complete ratings every 25 minutes based on their classroom observations or videos of the classroom, and a total rating is averaged across the day. The CLASS also employs a 7-point Likert-type scale and has 14 items organized into subscales of emotional support, classroom organization, and instructional support. In subsequent elaborations, developers have designed different versions of the CLASS for infant, toddler, pre-K, K–3, upper elementary, and secondary programs (https://teachstone.com).

ICP: Focus on Quality of Inclusive Classrooms   Extending the measurement of quality to children with disabilities included in early childhood education programs, Soukakou (2016) developed the ICP, which has a structural format similar to the ECERS. It consists of 12 items with a 7-point Likert-type rating scale, having descriptive indicators identified for the 1, 3, 5, and

7 ratings. Assessors base their rating on a classroom observation of 2 ½–3 hours, an interview with the lead teacher, and document analysis (e.g., IEP). The subscales in the ICP are adaptations, adult involvement in peer interaction, adult guidance of children's free-choice activities and play, conflict resolution, membership, relationships between adults and children, support for communication, adaptations of group activities, transitions between activities, feedback, family–professional partnerships, and monitoring children's learning. The ICP has good evidence of reliability and validity (Soukakou, 2012; Soukakou et al., 2016).

Quality of After-School Programs

As many as 20% of children who attend public schools also participate in after-school programs. There has been substantial interest in assessing quality because after-school programs, when of high quality, may have positive effects that extend beyond the public school experience (Kuperminc et al., 2019). In a review of quality assessment approaches conducted for *Child Trends*, Kahn et al. (2008) found 25 tools that practitioners could use to assess quality, including a version of the ECERS. A primary example is the Afterschool Program Practices Tool (APT, Tracy et al., 2012), which is the basis of a large system of program improvement conducted by the National Institute on Out of School Time at Wellesley University. (For more information, see *The Assessment of Afterschool Program Practices Tool (APT): Findings from the APT Validation Study* at the Wellesley Centers for Women web site: https://www.wcwonline.org/vmfiles/apt_report_v3 _final_6-30-20123.pdf.) The APT is based on observations in programs and staff questionnaires. The scale provides information about learning and skill building, program organization and structure, and supportive social environments.

Program Quality for Children and Youth With Autism

Assessment of program quality for individuals with autism has been more limited than the active assessment efforts in early childhood education and after-school programs, although some rating scales have been developed. Researchers have created several scales for the assessment of educational programs. For schools in Belgium, Renty and Roeyers (2005) developed a questionnaire to examine special education and inclusive school programs in which children with autism participated. The questionnaire was completed by school staff and provided information about services available, modification of the school environment, staff knowledge of autism, and parent involvement. The authors did not, however, provide information about the psychometric qualities of their questionnaire, and there have been no reports of its use in the United States. For the state of New York, Crimmins et al. (2001) developed the Autism Program Quality Indicators. This scale provides information about program (e.g., personnel, curriculum, family involvement) and student factors (e.g., assessment, transitions) (Librera et al., 2004). Yet, no information is available about its reliability and validity. The Professional Development in Autism (n.d.) program, funded from 2002 to 2007, developed the PDA Program Assessment to measure quality in programs for learners with autism. Although it provides useful information for service providers, the scale is a checklist containing items representing eight domains, and no evidence of reliability or validity has been reported for this measure. Similarly, several state committees (Colorado Department of Education, 2016; Kansas State Department of Education, Special Education Services, 2013) have developed assessments of quality programs, often intended for teacher self-study of their programs, with none providing psychometric information.

Van Bourgondien et al. (1998) developed the Environmental Rating Scale (ERS), which is a staff-administered rating scale designed to assess the quality of residential programs providing services to adolescents and adults with autism. The authors have published evidence of reliability and construct validity, although only 52 adolescents and adults with autism participated in the study. In a revision of the ERS, Hubel et al. (2008) developed a questionnaire version of the scale, the ERS-Q, which could be completed by program staff. They found high internal consistency and substantial concurrent validity between the two scales, although again the number of participants in the study was quite low ($n = 18$). Again, the authors used this scale to assess out-of-school/residential settings for adolescents and young adults rather than school-based programs across the grade range.

In summary, although a variety of measures of program quality have been developed, they generally lack the psychometric evidence of reliability and validity that professionals commonly expect in assessments. The exception is the ERS-Q, which, while having some evidence of reliability and validity, was designed for use in residential settings for adults with autism rather than school-based programs for children with autism.

APERS DEVELOPMENT

This section discusses the role of the National Professional Development Center on Autism (NPDC) in developing the APERS, the conceptual framework underlying the APERS, and the process of developing this instrument.

Role of the NPDC

In 2007, the Office of Special Education Programs (OSEP), U.S. Department of Education funded the NPDC. (For more information, visit the NPDC web site: https://autismpdc.fpg.unc.edu/national -professional-development-center-autism-spectrum-disorder.) OSEP's intent was to promote teachers' and other service providers' use of evidence-based practices in educational programs for children and youth with autism. Professional development at the state level was the process through which such changes in teacher behavior would occur, and NPDC's specific mission was to design a model of professional development that states could employ.

At that time, there were two significant challenges to such a task. The first challenge was that there had not been a comprehensive, systematic review of the autism intervention literature than identified evidence-based practices. During its early years, NPDC staff did such a review and initially identified 24 practices from studies published between 1996 and 2006 and met stringent methodological criteria (Odom et al., 2010). Five years later, the team published an update of this review, increasing the publication years covered to 1990–2011 and identifying 27 evidence-based practices (Wong et al., 2015). A third review that incorporates the intervention literature from 1990 to 2017 was published (Steinbrenner et al., 2020) through the National Clearinghouse on Autism Evidence and Practice (NCAEP; https://ncaep.fpg.unc.edu) and also has come out in a refereed journal article (Hume et al., 2021).

Although identifying evidence-based practices was an essential step in the process, a more fundamental second challenge existed. The previous school-based work of investigators who made up the NPDC team indicated that quite a range of quality exists in programs for children with autism. Some programs were characterized by the absence of a predictable schedule, disorganization in the room arrangement, a negative social climate, infrequent use of validated curriculum materials, dysfunctional interdisciplinary teaming, and alienation of parents. These features did not characterize all programs, but in our experience, they occurred often enough in schools to be a problem. Trying to implement evidence-based practices in programs that did not have a sufficient foundation of program quality would be an exercise in futility.

For NPDC, whose mission was to increase teachers' use of evidence-based practices, there was a great need for an assessment of program quality that could generate information schools could use to increase the quality of their programs and provide a stable and facilitative foundation for the implementation of evidence-based practices. There was, however, no conceptual framework for elements of educational programs that reflected quality, nor was there a reliable and valid way to assess it. To address this barrier/limitation in the field, NPDC investigators and their colleagues took on the task of developing a reliable and valid assessment of autism program quality, which became the APERS. The original APERS assessment was developed to evaluate program quality in preschool and elementary programs, as described next; this assessment was later modified for use in evaluating middle and high school programs.

Conceptual Framework of the APERS

The quality of programs for children and youth with autism consists of multiple dimensions (see Figure 1.1). There are a variety of central domains that we call, as a group, *program ecology*. These consist of structural features of the programs such as learning environment, structure and schedule, and positive social climate; assessment practices; general instructional practices; intervention and instruction in specific learning content areas such as social competence, communication, and independence; and interventions for challenging or interfering behavior. The quality of preparation for postschool transition is important for middle and high school programs, so this feature was added to the APERS-MH. In addition to program ecology, the collaborative and planful ways in which an interdisciplinary team works together are an important feature of program quality, as is the school's relationship with and involvement of the family.

Development Process for the APERS

Development of the APERS began with the creation of the preschool/elementary program rating scale. Beginning in 2007, NPDC investigators followed a systematic and iterative instrument development process. The first step was to review the literature on assessment of program and learning environments for children and youth who are typically developing and for individuals with autism. From this review, NPDC investigators located and reviewed similar scales, adapting items that appeared to appropriately reflect aspects of program quality for children and youth with autism. We also created applicable items, sorted items into conceptual categories, shared analyses with other members of the team, revised items based on feedback, and assembled items into domains. When NPDC team members had identified the initial set of items, they then wrote item anchors (i.e., descriptions of the classroom or practice necessary to code an item rating), shared anchors with other team members for review, and revised item anchors based on feedback.

The items and domains were assembled into the APERS Preschool/Elementary (APERS-PE) version. Investigators then shared the APERS-PE with a team of experts and practitioners in middle school and high school programs for learners with autism and modified it to create the middle/high school version, APERS Middle/High School (APERS-MH). Items were revised to represent the different quality features of middle/high school programs.

NPDC research team members then pilot tested the APERS in preschool, elementary, middle, and high school programs for learners with autism in public schools in one school district. Pilot test information was used to revise observation and data collection procedures as well as individual items. Both versions of the APERS were then distributed to the research staff at the three sites of the NPDC (North Carolina, Wisconsin, California). Staff administered the APERS in the fall of 2008 and spring of 2009 in early childhood, elementary, and middle/high school programs. These staff members provided detailed feedback about items and data collection procedures, which were incorporated into the 2011 versions of the APERS.

In 2015, the U.S. Department of Education-Institute of Education Sciences (IES) funded The Efficacy Study on Elementary Learners with Autism (TESELA; R324A150047) project as a randomized control trial to determine the efficacy of the NPDC model when implemented in elementary schools in a southeastern state. This research study also required the APERS-PE to reflect the whole school quality rather than single classroom quality. The TESELA research team made similar modifications as had occurred previously for the high school APERS.

Last, an APERS workgroup team was assembled in 2018–2019 to review all the current versions of the APERS. Team members corrected or modified discrepancies in wording and made sure that items for the preschool/elementary and middle/high school versions were comparable. For the APERS-MH, the scale was revised to establish a separate postschool transition domain.

APERS 2023

The current versions of the APERS are the culmination of more than 15 years of research with the instrument. The APERS-PE consists of 62 items organized into 10 domains. The APERS-MH consists of 69 items organized in 11 domains, with the additional domain and items primarily focusing on the transition out of school and preparation for post-secondary employment and/or education. Items within each domain are further grouped by dimensions (e.g., Safety and Organization of Learning Environments are dimensions within the Learning Environments domain). The items and domains for the two versions of the APERS are in Figure 1.2.

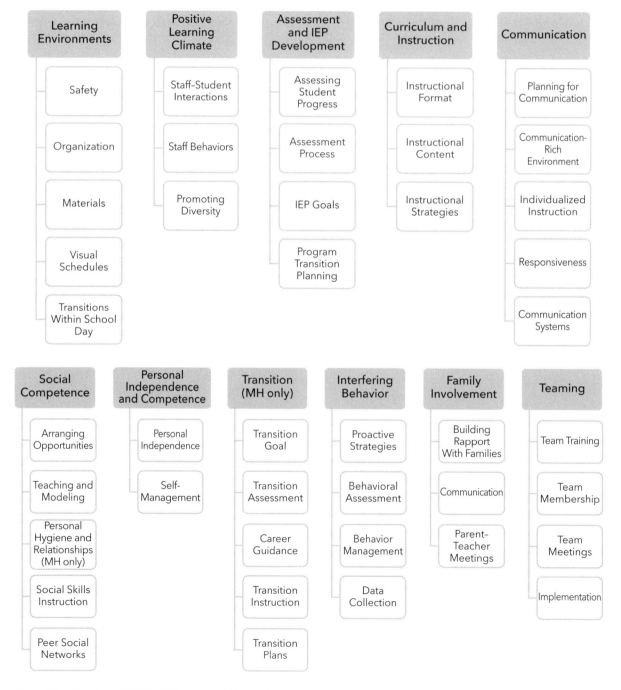

Figure 1.2. Domains of APERS and dimensions within domains.

Curriculum and Instruction			Show/Hide All Contents	
Instructional Format	Item #21 (O)		Score	
1	3		5	
All team members use only one instructional format (e.g., teacher-led, student-led, small group, large group, one-on-one).	One team member uses at least two instructional formats (e.g., teacher-led, student-led, small group, large group, one-on-one).		Most team members use a variety of instructional formats (e.g., teacher-led, student-led, small group, large group, one-on-one).	
Team members do not match most instructional formats with individual student needs.	One team member matches instructional formats to individual student needs most of the time.		Most team members match instructional formats to individual student needs most of the time.	
Team members do not match most instructional formats with instructional content.	One team member matches instructional formats to instructional content most of the time.		Most team members match instructional formats to instructional content most of the time.	

Figure 1.3. Sample APERS item.

A sample assessment item from the Scoring Tool is shown in Figure 1.3. Items in the APERS follow a 5-point Likert-type format; more information and directions about rating an item appear in Chapter 3. Table 1.1 lists item numbers for each domain and dimensions within each. As previously mentioned, the assessor observes in the classroom of program, interviews relevant staff members, and reviews relevant documents such as the IEP. More specific directions about collecting these data are provided in Chapter 2. Detailed explanation of scoring is presented in Chapter 3.

Table 1.1. Comparing domains, dimensions, and items on the APERS-PE and APERS-MH

Domain	Dimensions	APERS-PE	APERS-MH
Learning Environments	Safety	1–3	1–3
	Organization of Learning Environments	4–5	4–6
	Materials	6–7	7–8
	Visual Schedules	8	9
	Transitions Within the School Day	9	10
Positive Learning Climate	Staff–Student Interactions	10–11	11
	Staff Behaviors	12–13	12–13
	Promoting Diversity	14	14
Assessment and IEP Development	Assessing Student Progress	15–16	15–16
	IEP Goals	17–19	17–19
	Program Transition Planning	20	20
Curriculum and Instruction	Instructional Format	21, 26	21, 26
	Instructional Content	22, 25	22, 25
	Instructional Strategies	23–24, 27–32	23–24, 27–32
Communication	Planning for Communication	33	33
	Communication-Rich Environment	34	34
	Individualized Communication Instruction	35	35
	Responsiveness to Student Communication	36	36
	Communication Systems	37	37

(continued)

Table 1.1. *(continued)*

Domain	Dimensions	APERS-PE	APERS-MH
Social Competence	Arranging Opportunities	38–39	38–39
	Teaching and Modeling	40	40
	Puberty and Relationships	–	41
	Social Skills Instruction	41	42
	Peer Social Networks	42	43
Personal Independence and Competence	Personal Independence	43–45	44–45
	Self-Management	46	46–47
Post-Secondary Transition Planning	Transition Goals	–	48
	Transition Assessment	–	49
	Career Guidance	–	50
	Transition Instruction	–	51
	Transition Plans	–	52–53
Interfering Behavior	Proactive Strategies	47	54
	Behavioral Assessment	48–49	55–56
	Behavior Management	50	57
	Data Collection	51	58
Family Involvement	Building Rapport With Families	52	59
	Communication	53–54	60–61
	Parent-Teacher Meetings	55	62
Teaming	Team Training	56	63
	Team Membership	57–59	64–66
	Team Meetings	60–61	67–68
	Implementation	62	69

As previously noted, we have developed an optional self-rating scale for teachers and other service providers designed to produce information that can be used internally (e.g., by the teacher or other school staff) for program improvement. More information about this scale and directions for completing it are included in Chapter 4. In Chapter 5, we describe the ways in which APERS information can be used by different groups, such as policy makers or administrators, school-level leaders, and individual teachers or other service providers. The psychometric information about reliability and validity of the APERS, as well as the use of the APERS in research, is reported in Chapter 6.

SUMMARY

The APERS-PE provides information about the quality of programs for children with autism enrolled in preschool and elementary classroom programs. It draws on observations, interviews, and reviews of written records and yields ratings of the program domains that make up overall quality. This information can then be used by program leaders to address quality challenges for their programs as well as highlight program quality strengths.

2 Getting Started
APERS Training and Administration

"There are two mistakes one can make along the road to truth—not going
all the way, and not starting."
—Buddha

"What's well begun is half done."
—Horace

The APERS assessment requires that the rater gathers information by

- Observing in the classroom or school

- Reviewing the IEP(s) and other relevant records

- Interviewing staff and at least one of the student's parents

These three sources of information all contribute to scoring items, as will be described in the next chapter. These actions require some preparation ahead of time. The more prepared one is, the better the assessment will go. A flow chart for the data collection process appears in Figure 2.1.

After completing a preliminary interview to make arrangements, the rater identifies the student(s) with autism who will be the focus of the assessment process. The APERS may provide information about an individual classroom (e.g., a self-contained classroom), a program (e.g., the inclusive program within a school), or the whole school. When conducting a classroom-based APERS (e.g. self-contained classroom), select two students with autism as focal students. For program-level APERS (inclusive programs or self-contained programs), select two to three students. Students should be selected across different classrooms and represent different ages/grade levels and development. For school-based APERS, a minimum of three students should be selected and represent students in both inclusive and self-contained settings (one student within a self-contained program and two students within an inclusive program). The rater reviews the student's or students' records before observing in the classroom or school. Following the observation, the rater completes information-gathering interviews with staff and the families of the focal students.

If possible, raters should have completed APERS training before completing the APERS. It provides a thorough introduction to the APERS-PE items and indicators in each domain. Raters who are unable to participate in APERS training should review the APERS-PE Scoring Tool (see Getting Started in Figure 2.2) to familiarize themselves with the items and indicators in each domain before administering the APERS-PE.

A one-page Record Review Guide and an Observer Guide are included with the APERS-PE. These reproducible forms are provided as Appendices 2.1 and 2.2 and are also available via the

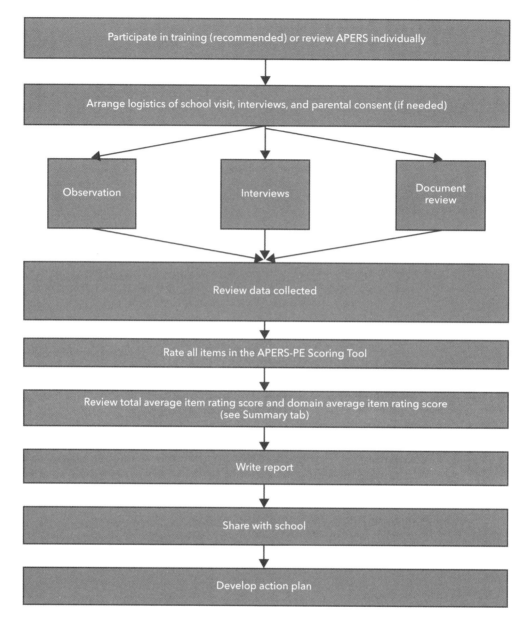

Figure 2.1. Flowchart for APERS assessment process.

Brookes Download Hub. Raters should keep these guides on hand for quick reference while conducting the review of student records and the classroom observation. Raters should have available a means of taking notes during these steps. (To ensure raters remain inconspicuous during classroom observation, pen-and-paper notetaking is preferable to typing on a computer.) The APERS-PE kit also includes protocol forms for conducting a preliminary interview and interviews with school team members and parents. Raters should use these forms to guide their questioning and take notes during the interviews. Reproducible copies of the fillable PDF forms are available via the Brookes Download Hub.

APERS-PE Tool Guide

Overview

The Autism Program Environment Rating Scale Preschool/Elementary (APERS-PE) Scoring Tool is designed to automatically calculate APERS scores and create graphics that convey the summary scores.

The APERS employs a Likert-type rating scale consisting of five rating options. Ratings or scores for each item are generated by the Scoring Tool. Based on the indicators the rater marks in the Scoring Tool, each item is automatically scored a 1, 2, 3, 4, or 5. An item score of 1 or 2 represents poor quality, an item score of 3 represents acceptable quality, and an item score of 4 or 5 represents high quality.

There are quality indicators for the 1, 3, and 5 ratings for each item in the Scoring Tool, which the rater judges as present or absent. APERS-PE items are rated based on data collected from classroom observations and interviews with school staff and with parent(s) of the focal child(ren) observed, as well as document review. The rater should be familiar with the items on the APERS-PE Scoring Tool before conducting the APERS, and previous training when possible is advised. The rater should also have the following guidance documents available while conducting the APERS-PE:

- **APERS-PE Observer Guide:** Things to Remember to Look For
- **APERS-PE Interview Protocols**
- **APERS-PE Record Review Guide:** Things to Remember to Look For

Figure 2.2. Getting Started tab of the APERS-PE Scoring Tool.

Tip boxes for each step of the process are included throughout this chapter; also, a complete APERS Tip Sheet is included in Appendix 2.3 for the rater's convenience. The following sections explain APERS training and administration step by step.

STEP 1: COMPLETE APERS TRAINING

The first step is for the rater to participate in APERS training, if possible. Training is strongly recommended because it introduces the rater to the terminology established for specific assessment features, highlights the aspects of the program environment reflected in each domain, conveys the interpretation of items established by the assessment developers, and provides opportunities for asking questions.

Arrange to Participate in APERS Training

APERS training is provided through Frank Porter Graham Child Development Institute (FPG) at the University of North Carolina at Chapel Hill. For information about training availability and scheduling, the reader can go to The National Clearinghouse on Autism Research and Practice (https://ncaep.fpg.unc.edu) or inquire through the Brookes Publishing web site (https://brookespublishing.com).

The training process includes an initial 8 hours of didactic training that includes an introduction and overview of the APERS, training on administering APERS, APERS video practice, and preparation for observations. Participants will arrange to complete their own APERS at a local school. Following administering the APERS, participants will meet with APERS trainers to review scoring. A didactic 3-hour group training will provide information on the debrief and professional development planning process. Finally, participants will have the opportunity for individual follow-up meetings with trainers to review a report and answer questions about scoring.

Conduct and Score an APERS With an Experienced Trainer

Such training includes a description of all domains, dimensions, and items and particularly the way in which items should be interpreted and coded. The training should also include at least one practice session and one session conducting an APERS with a person who had previously been trained to administer the assessment and to compare scoring after data has been collected and item ratings completed. Agreement on item ratings is conducted at this stage, and the new rater and experienced rater should reach a consensus on discrepancies. The last phase of this training is for the new rater to complete a second APERS on their own and share the ratings and assessment with the experienced rater. At that point, the new rater can pose questions that may have come up during the assessment.

Study APERS Independently if You Cannot Participate in Training

For some users, it may not be possible to attend a training. In such cases, it is especially important for the new rater to review the entire APERS assessment, reading each item to make sure that the information collected from the classroom(s) allows the rater to complete the rating. APERS training will provide just such an introduction, but if training has not occurred, then this type of self-study is essential for the planning.

Anticipate Logistics for Collecting Data

As previously mentioned, the APERS may be collected to assess quality of a single classroom or a program within a school. Data collection logistics may be less complicated for a self-contained program that involves one or two classrooms in a school than for programs in which children with autism are included in the general education curriculum for part or all of the day, or ones in which they change classes during the day. For example, in elementary schools offering inclusive programs, there may be children with autism in different grades and classes that may require the rater to observe in multiple classrooms. Also, if there are inclusive programs in middle and high schools, then students with autism will be changing classes, so the rater will need to distribute their observations across students and classes. More information about these different logistic requirements is provided in a subsequent section.

STEP 2: MAKE INITIAL ARRANGEMENTS FOR THE APERS

Before any actions related to the APERS occur in the school, it is essential that the school administration (principal and staff) know and agree to the APERS data collection and also be available for an interview. A sample letter to the key administrator in the school is included in Appendix 2.4.

Identify a Key School Contact Person

When APERS raters are from outside the school staff, which is most often the case, they should identify a school staff member who can assist. The responsibility of this key school contact person will be to make sure that school staff members know the rater will be observing in their class (and when they will be observing), arrange the time and location where the interviews will be conducted, and arrange for the rater to have access to representative students' IEPs.

Conduct the Preliminary Interview

It is helpful to conduct an initial preliminary interview with a key staff member before the observations begin. The protocol for conducting the APERS-PE Preliminary Interview appears in Figure 2.3. During this preliminary interview, the key school staff member gives the APERS rater a tour of the school. In this walk-through, the school contact person shows the rater the various features of the school (e.g., geographic arrangement of classrooms), lunch room, gym, playground for recess. Receiving a map of the school, if available, is also very helpful. A planning guide for the APERS-PE is included in Appendix 2.5.

Obtain Informed Consent From Parents

As part of the APERS assessment, the rater will observe several students (called *focal students*) during a school day, read their IEP(s), and potentially interview their parents. If the APERS rater is from outside the school system, the parents would usually need to provide consent for the rater to gain access to focal students' IEPs and other written documents. This really depends on local school district policies. Similarly, if the APERS rater is a school staff member or employee of the school district, then they

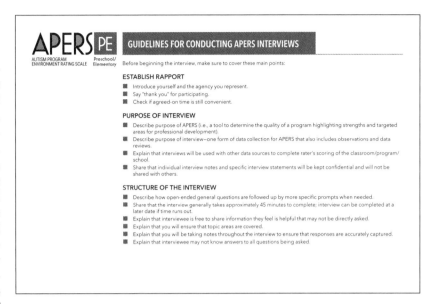

Figure 2.3. Protocol for conducting the Preliminary Interview.

should follow their district policy in obtaining parental consent. During this consenting process, it is also a good time to request an interview with the parent(s) and arrange a time and place. A sample letter for the parent is included in Appendix 2.6.

Plan for Classroom Observations

The rater(s) should plan for at least one full day for observations in the program. It will be important to observe the program environments in which each focal student participates for approximately 3 hours during the day. If the program is within a single classroom, then the rater can spread observations among activities or program environments occurring for each of two children (e.g., individual instructional activities, group activities, lunch, recess). If the program is in different classrooms (e.g., a special education program having two classes, an inclusive program in which children are in multiple general education classes), then the rater can move among different children, activities, and classrooms.

The purpose of the observations is to obtain a picture of the overall program, which requires observations in a variety of environments (e.g., resource/special education classroom, general education classroom, special). This is why it is necessary to plan observational "samples" across broad educational environments, rather than a small number of activities with an individual student and single teacher or staff member.

STEP 3A: REVIEW IEPs AND OTHER RELEVANT STUDENT RECORDS

The IEP and, if applicable, behavioral intervention plans (BIPs) contain important information about the quality of the program planned for the student. The rater should arrange to review these documents for the identified focal students prior to the observation. By reviewing these IEPs and other relevant student records, the rater will be able to observe whether specific goals are being implemented in classrooms and score APERS-PE items that focus on the development of IEPs.

These documents vary widely by school districts. At a minimum, they should include information about the current functioning of the student, possibly assessment information, individualized goals, objectives or benchmarks written in an observable and measurable

APERS-PE Record Review Guide: Things to Remember to Look For	
Domain	**Things to look for**
Assessment and IEP Development	• Data collection methods (format, relevant information, student involvement)
	• Family participation in IEP meetings and IEP development
	• IEP goals and objectives reflect assessment data, are observable, are measurable, address core deficits of autism and additional areas as appropriate
Curriculum and Instruction	• Goals capitalize on students' strengths and interest
Communication	• Assessment of communication needs
Interfering Behavior*	• Review functional behavioral assessments (FBAs) if available (hypotheses and replacement behaviors)
	• Review behavioral intervention plans (BIPs) developed if needed (assessment of current skills, strategies for teaching replacement behaviors)
	• Collection of data on interfering behavior
Teaming	• Multidisciplinary team provide services
	• All team members (included families) invited to team meetings and part of decision-making team
	• Related services identified in IEPs, and scheduled services are provided

*For students who have the level of interfering behavior that requires a behavioral intervention plan.

Figure 2.4. Record Review Guide.

format, the placement of the student (e.g., amount of time in general education) and related services provided (e.g., the amount of speech therapy service per week). The one-page Record Review Guide (Figure 2.4) provides reminders of what to look for during this document review and is organized by the relevant APERS domains.

If possible, it is helpful for the rater to have the IEP with them during the observations and interviews. Interview questions marked by an "R" must be scored by IEP review if adequate information is available. Otherwise, the information can be obtained through interviews (I) with teachers, parents, or team members. If IEPs are available only for review and copies are not available, then the rater should make notes of the goals and objectives identified as well as the other essential elements of the IEPs previously mentioned.

In addition to the IEPs and transition plans, the rater may read or obtain copies of other documents that might inform their ratings. Examples of these may be data sheets for students, description of the program provided to parents, teacher's note(s) home to parents, school description of a "best buddies" program, and so forth. The rater may use this information when completing the APERS ratings.

■ Tips for Record Review

1. Ask for the opportunity to review records in advance.
   - Recent IEPs
   - Data related to IEP goals
   - Functional behavioral assessment (FBA) (if applicable)
   - Behavioral intervention plan (BIP) (if applicable)
2. Know what permissions and access you will need.
3. Have the Record Review guide on hand as a reminder of what to look for.

STEP 3B: CONDUCT OBSERVATIONS

The purposes of the observations are to gather information about structural (i.e., layout, arrangement of space) and organizational (e.g., schedule, routines, consistency) features of the classroom(s), the interactions of the school staff with the students in the classrooms, and the types of curriculum materials and intervention practices that school staff are using. Raters should plan to spend at least 3–6 hours in observations and distribute their observations across the different settings in which students participate.

Observe a Variety of Environments

Before beginning the observation, raters should review students' schedules to ensure that a variety of environments are included in the observation. We recommend that the rater observe the primary classroom activities for a period of time (e.g., opening, academics, language), transitions between classes, special activities in which students may engage (e.g., music, art, library), recess or physical education, and lunch. The rater may use their judgment about how long to spend observing in a setting based on the information that is needed and the redundancy of activities in the setting. For example, if a rater has been in a class for a period of time, has noted the structural features of the class, has seen transitions between activities or phases of a lesson, and has observed multiple student interactions with teachers and/or peers, then the observation may have reached a point of saturation (i.e., little new will be learned by more time in observation). At that point, the rater can make a judgment about moving on to another setting or observe another student.

Let the Focal Student(s) Guide Observations

Raters should base their ratings on the quality of the general program environment, but it is overwhelming to try to observe everything at once. It is helpful to identify two to three students (i.e., depending whether assessment is of a class or program/school) to guide the rater's observations. These should be students who represent the range of functioning levels in the classroom or program. By guiding the observations, the rater may switch their observations from one student to another as they participate in different activities and interact with different staff members. When observing these focal students, the rater may observe things happening with other children with autism in the class or program as well, and that information may be factored into their assessment ratings. When planning the interviews, it will be helpful, although not essential, to speak with the related services providers or other school staff providing services to one or more of the students being observed.

Observe on a Typical School Day

The rater should observe only when the students' primary teacher is present on the day of the observation and should reschedule the observation if a substitute teacher is responsible for the class for the day. It is important to avoid observing when there are special events occurring for the day (e.g., a field day that takes a good part of the morning), days before holiday breaks, or days that are otherwise atypical (e.g., end of the year testing and preparation days leading up to it).

Take Notes While Observing

Because the APERS is a rating scale rather than a time-based observational measure in which the observer records events when they occur or using a time-interval (e.g., during a 10-second period), a rating is based on summary judgments about features of the program environment. The two-page Observer Guide (Figure 2.5) provides reminders of what to look for during observation and is organized by the 10 APERS-PE domains. It is helpful for the rater to take notes on the features of the program that they observe. Some raters take copious written notes about the classrooms and instruction while they are observing, whereas others write down short phrases to remind them of what they observed. The type of notes recorded are at the discretion of the rater, and their function is to serve as a reminder of what happened in a specific setting or activity. Because the rater may be observing in several different settings and several different students, such notes aid the rater in basing their item rating on their observation.

Be Inconspicuous

It is important to be a "fly on the wall" when observing in classroom or other school settings. The rater should attempt to be as inconspicuous as possible. We strongly recommend arranging the best location for the rater ahead of time. In most cases, the rater should refrain from

APERS-PE Observer Guide: Things to Remember to Look For	
Domain	**Things to look for**
Learning Environments	• Safety (hazards absent, hygienic, staff supervision) • Space well organized for learning and independence, adequacy of materials, visual supports • Visual supports for promoting independence • Transitions (between activity and classes)
Positive Learning Climate	• Affective quality (positive/negative) of interactions between staff and students • Staff focus on students' engagement and learning • Cultural diversity in materials and interactions
Assessment and IEP Development	• Data collected on student performance (related to IEP) • Data collected related to student's IEP goals
Curriculum and Instruction	• Clarity and appropriateness (length of learning activity, prompting, reinforcement) • Instruction related to IEP • Variety of instructional formats • Visual supports • Task analysis • Accommodations (sensory or levels of support)
Communication	• Opportunities to communicate with staff and peers • Staff responsiveness to student communication • Specific instruction/interventions to promote communication (if appropriate) • Use of augmentative and alternative communication (AAC) systems (if appropriate)
Social Competence	• Informal and/or teacher-planned opportunities for interaction with peers (e.g., organized play or recess, peer social networks) • Specific intervention/instruction to promote social skills or social engagement (if appropriate) • Staff model of good social skills • Instruction related to hygiene

Figure 2.5.   Observer Guide.

talking with the teacher during teaching times, although when there is a break, the rater might ask questions about the purpose of an activity if it was unclear. Natural times often occur during the day for conversation outside of the teaching context or classroom (e.g., when elementary teachers are monitoring their students during recess). There are times when children may try to interact with the rater, in which case the rater should either ignore the student or just say, "I am working now and can't talk." Also, it is very helpful if the rater has identifying "signage," such as a badge with name and organization or an ID worn on a lanyard. Schools usually will require that observers check in at the office and will provide a badge indicating that the observer is an official visitor, which may be sufficient for self-identification.

Observer Cautions: Preventing, Intervening in, and Reporting Harmful Situations

The rater should never be left alone with the students in a class or assume supervisory responsibilities for students. If a student being observed is in a situation in which they might be harmed, then the rater should alert that teacher or teaching assistant about the situation. The rater should intervene to prevent the harmful situation from occurring only as a last resort but should not hesitate if necessary. Although it rarely occurs, if the rater observes instances of abuse or potential abuse, then it is their ethical responsibility to report such instances to their supervisor.

▓ Tips for Observation

1. Become familiar with observation items beforehand.

2. Have the Observer Guide on hand during observation to remind you of what to look for.

3. Find a way to take notes unobtrusively (not on a computer).

4. Ask teachers to guide your behavior (e.g., toward students with interfering behavior, if students approach).

5. Scan the environment.

6. Move around as negotiated with teacher.

7. Focus on students with autism.

8. Find opportunities when you can explore the environment more thoroughly (e.g., when children leave their desks).

9. Look for missed opportunities for using evidence-based practices or promoting children's goals.

10. Observe all team members.

STEP 3C: COMPLETE INTERVIEWS

Because observations may occur on only 1–2 days of a school year, it is impossible to observe all features of the program that would indicate quality. Interviews are designed to obtain information about program features that cannot be observed directly. In the APERS-PE Scoring Tool, items based on interview information are designated by an "I".

As noted, the Preliminary Interview is conducted at the beginning of the administration process. It is most useful for the other interviews to occur after the observations, which allows the rater to ask questions, if needed, about things that may have come up during the observations, as well as questions about features of the program that cannot be observed (e.g., committee meeting, teaming collaboration, family participation).

Determine Whom to Interview

Again, the interviews are designed to obtain representative information about the school program. School personnel who provide educational services for students in the program should be included. In an inclusive program, these individuals would include

- The students' special education or resource teacher(s) (i.e., the teacher who spends the most time with the students)

- One or more general education teachers if they regularly see the student (e.g., physical education teacher, general education teacher)

- One team member who delivers related services (preferably an SLP)

- A key administrator (e.g., principal, assistant principal, special education program chair lead in large schools)

- One parent (the parents of the focal children observed for whom an IEP was available and has been reviewed)

In a self-contained program, these individuals would include

- The teacher in the self-contained classroom

- One team member who delivers related services (preferably an SLP)

- A general education teacher if children are in general education classes for part of the day or if the teacher is responsible for specials (e.g., art, music)

- A key administrator (e.g., principal, assistant principal, special education program chair lead in large schools)

- One parent (the parent of the focal child observed for whom an IEP was available and has been reviewed)

Study the Interview Protocols and Questions

The APERS-PE includes protocols for the interviews with special education teachers, general education teachers, SLPs, administrators, and family members. The rater should use the special education teacher interview protocol for other related services personnel. Raters should familiarize themselves with the interview protocols before the interview (see Figure 2.6).

The interview questions are generally organized by the domains of the APERS-PE. Each of the interview questions is referenced to an item or items of the APERS-PE. (See the example from the Special Educator interview protocol shown in Figure 2.7.) The questions shown here address the Learning Environments domain, specifically the Safety and Transitions Within the School Day

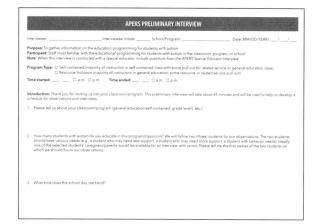

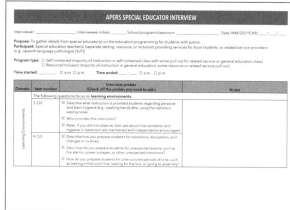

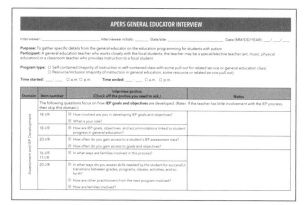

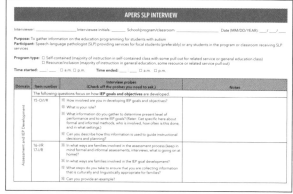

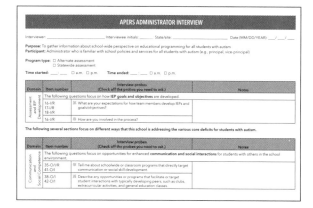

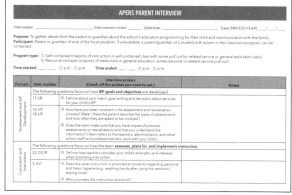

Figure 2.6. Protocols for conducting the Preliminary Interview, Special Educator Interview, General Educator Interview, Speech-Language Pathologist Interview, Administrator Interview, and Parent Interview.

dimensions. The first three questions correspond to Item 3 about hygiene and sanitation as part of safety. The latter three questions correspond to Item 9 about transitions within the day.

Conduct the Interviews

Raters do not have to ask all the questions verbatim; they may rephrase the question in their own words if it will elicit the needed information. Also, if the rater already has the information from an observation or previous interview, then they may skip that question. The interview protocols have space for taking notes. The notes would summarize the information provided by the interviewee rather than verbatim responses.

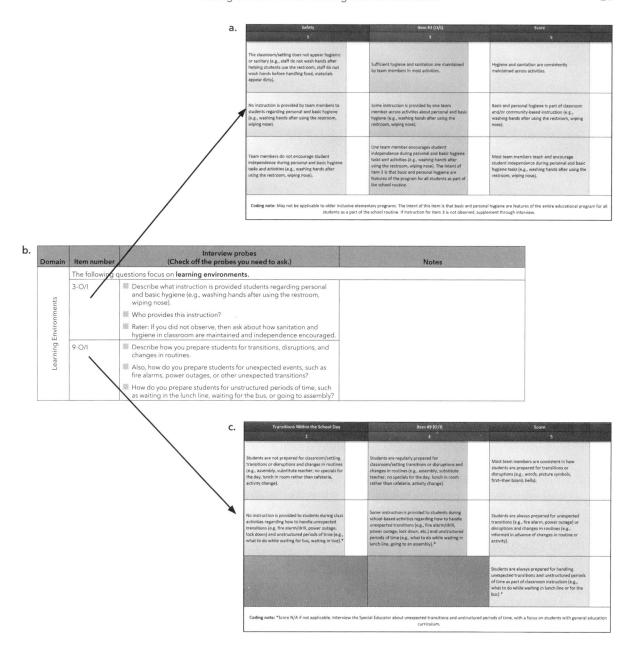

Figure 2.7. Sample interview question from the Special Educator Interview Protocol.

The rater should assure the individual being interviewed that the information provided will be private and not shared directly with anyone else. The interviews should take place in a private location to ensure privacy. Conducting face-to-face interviews is preferable. This may not always be possible for some school staff, however, because of schedules or remote learning arrangements during the COVID-19 pandemic. Parents also may have difficulty traveling to the school for interviews. In those cases, telephone or other telecommunication (i.e., Skype, Face-time, Zoom) interviews may be the feasible option.

▨ Tips for Interviews

1. If you cannot observe indicators for an item, then ask about these during the interview.
2. Cover the topics in the interview protocols, but the interview does not have to be in order.
3. Once you have enough information needed to score an item, you can stop asking about it.
4. For scoring: When interview information conflicts with information from
    -   Other interviewees—score based on professional judgment
    -   Observations—score based on observation
    -   Records—score based on records

Additional scoring tips are provided in Chapter 3.

ADDITIONAL CONSIDERATIONS FOR SELF-CONTAINED SPECIAL EDUCATION CLASSES AND INCLUSIVE PROGRAMS

In a single school, students with autism often may be enrolled in a self-contained special education program with one or two classes or an inclusive program with multiple classes in the school. The distinction between these programs is how much of the student's school day is spent in general education classes.

Special Education Classes

Students in special education classes spend most of their day in a class with other students who have disabilities, and the special education teacher is the teacher responsible for the students' program. There may be times during the day when students are in other special classes (e.g., music, art, technology lab), specially arranged activities with typically developing peers, or general education classes for a relatively short period of time. As noted, the rater should arrange to observe in all of those contexts.

Inclusive Programs

Preschool and elementary school students who are in inclusive programs are enrolled in and spend most of their time in a general education class with their typically developing peers. Depending on the school arrangement, the students may be in one class for most of the day with the same teacher and possibly assistants, or they may change classes for some activities (e.g., one teacher teaches literacy, so students from all the third grades in the school go to that teacher's class at some point to participate in literacy instruction). In these programs, the general education and special education teachers share responsibilities for the students' program. The general education teacher is responsible for instruction related to the general education curriculum as well as implementing individual instruction and accommodations as needed for the student(s) with autism in their class. The special education teacher is usually responsible for the IEP and individualized goals and objectives, consulting or collaborating with the general education teacher for making needed accommodations for the student with autism, possibly providing push-in support in the classroom, and possibly providing pull-out instruction for the student for a relatively small proportion of the day. Because students with autism in the inclusive program will be in multiple classes, the rater should observe two to three students with autism in the different classes and in educational contexts (e.g., general education instruction, resource room pull out if it occurs). The rater will have to judge the number of students who need to be observed to give a represented sample of the contexts.

The APERS was designed to assess quality of programs for children and youth with autism in community public school settings. In some locations, services for children with autism may be in special education schools that only include students with disabilities. The information generated by the APERS could also be useful for such programs. It is, however, important to note that a few items on the APERS specify that opportunities for social interaction and communication with typically developing students occur, so these special education schools may score lower than the community-based schools because of these items' ratings. In interpreting the APERS results for separate special education schools that are not inclusive, the users should just be aware of this feature of the assessment.

If the purpose of the APERS assessment is to gather quality information on the specific inclusive or special education program, then scoring a single APERS rating would obviously be appropriate. If the purpose of the APERS assessment is to obtain a schoolwide evaluation of the quality of the program for students with autism in which there are separate primarily self-contained, special education and inclusive programs, then the rater should complete separate APERS for both types of programs.

SUMMARY

In this chapter, we have provided advice for how to collect the information needed for completing the APERS ratings, which is described in detail in Chapter 3. We are not sure that we completely agree with Horace that "What's well begun is half done," but beginning well has considerable advantages. Spending time preparing for the APERS data collection in the schools will certainly pay off in efficiency of the data collection process, possibly the accuracy of the information collected, and certainly in reducing any frustrations that might emerge from a poorly organized school visit.

APERS-PE Record Review Guide: Things to Remember to Look For

Domain	Things to look for
Assessment and IEP Development	• Data collection methods (format, relevant information, student involvement) • Family participation in IEP meetings and IEP development • IEP goals and objectives reflect assessment data, are observable, are measurable, address core deficits of autism and additional areas as appropriate
Curriculum and Instruction	• Goals capitalize on students' strengths and interest
Communication	• Assessment of communication needs
Interfering Behavior[a]	• Review functional behavioral assessments (FBAs) if available (hypotheses and replacement behaviors) • Review behavioral intervention plans (BIPs) developed if needed (assessment of current skills, strategies for teaching replacement behaviors) • Collection of data on interfering behavior
Teaming	• Multidisciplinary team provide services • All team members (included families) invited to team meetings and part of decision-making team • Related services identified in IEPs, and scheduled services are provided

[a]For students who have the level of interfering behavior that requires a behavioral intervention plan.

Autism Program Environment Rating Scale–Preschool/Elementary (APERS-PE) by Samuel L. Odom, Ann M. Sam, and Ann W. Cox.
Copyright © 2024 by The University of North Carolina at Chapel Hill. All rights reserved. Published by Paul H. Brookes Publishing Co., Inc.

APERS-PE Observer Guide: Things to Remember to Look For

Domain	Things to look for
Learning Environments	• Safety (hazards absent, hygienic, staff supervision) • Space well organized for learning and independence, adequacy of materials, visual supports • Visual supports for promoting independence • Transitions (between activity and classes)
Positive Learning Climate	• Affective quality (positive/negative) of interactions between staff and students • Staff focus on students' engagement and learning • Cultural diversity in materials and interactions
Assessment and IEP Development	• Data collected on student performance (related to IEP) • Data collected related to student's IEP goals
Curriculum and Instruction	• Clarity and appropriateness (length of learning activity, prompting, reinforcement) • Instruction related to IEP • Variety of instructional formats • Visual supports • Task analysis • Accommodations (sensory or levels of support)
Communication	• Opportunities to communicate with staff and peers • Staff responsiveness to student communication • Specific instruction/interventions to promote communication (if appropriate) • Use of augmentative and alternative communication (AAC) systems (if appropriate)
Social Competence	• Informal and/or teacher-planned opportunities for interaction with peers (e.g., organized play or recess, peer social networks) • Specific intervention/instruction to promote social skills or social engagement (if appropriate) • Staff model of good social skills • Instruction related to hygiene

(continued)

Domain	Things to look for
Personal Independence and Competence	• Supports for independence (e.g., picture or digital schedules) • Opportunities for choice-making • Self-management or advocacy (e.g., requests help when needed) • Opportunities for sensory breaks (e.g., cool-down location)
Interfering Behavior	• Proactive strategies to prevent interfering behavior • Positive approaches (e.g., redirecting, ignoring) used in response to behavior • If needed, intervention plan in place and consistently followed • If intervention plan in place, data collected
Family Involvement	• Communication between school and home • Resources shared with family
Teaming	• Communication among team members (e.g., speech-language pathologist in the classroom, sharing information with classroom staff) • School staff participation in team meetings

APERS-PE Tip Sheet

RECORD REVIEW

- Ask for the opportunity to review records in advance.
  - Recent IEPs
  - Data related to IEP goals
  - Functional behavioral assessment (FBA) (if applicable)
  - Behavioral intervention plan (BIP) (if applicable)
  - Transition plan (if applicable)
- Know what permissions and access you will need.

OBSERVATION

- Become familiar with observation items beforehand by reviewing the APERS-PE Scoring Tool and the Observer Guide.
- Find a way to take notes unobtrusively (not on computer).
- Ask teachers to guide your behavior (e.g., toward students with interfering behavior, if students approach).
- Scan the environment.
- Move around as negotiated with teacher.
- Focus on students with autism.
- Find opportunities when you can explore the environment more thoroughly (e.g., when children leave their desks).
- Look for missed opportunities for instruction.
- Observe all team members.

INTERVIEWS

- Ask open-ended questions to gather specifics, such as "Give me an example…"
- If you cannot observe indicators for an item, then ask about these during the interview.
- Cover the topics in the interview protocols, but it does not have to be in order.
- Once you have enough information needed to score an item, you can stop asking about it.

SCORING

- During the scoring process, make note of overall themes and suggestions for debrief/report.
- Score based on the entire observation—not isolated interactions and occurrences.
- When interviewees conflict—score based on professional judgment.
- When interview conflicts with observation—score based on observation.
- When interview conflicts with records—score based on records.

Additional scoring tips are provided in Chapter 3.

(continued)

DEBRIEF

- Know your audience.

- Be a good coach.

- Share enough to motivate but not overwhelm.

- Give examples of strengths from observation, such as "We noticed when you did . . ."

- Give examples and/or resources with each opportunity for growth.

- Remember to not share specific information that could identify a team member's confidentiality.

Additional debriefing tips are provided in Chapter 4.

REPORT

- Be clear and concise.

- No more than three strengths/areas of concern.

- For each issue, provide observed example and suggested approach to address.

- For each strength, provide observed example.

- Know your audience—what do they need to hear in order to be open to the information?

- Provide graphs and explain them. (*Note:* If scores are very low [e.g., no domain is at the adequate level], you may use professional judgment to determine if appropriate to share graphs.)

Additional tips for writing the report are provided in Chapter 4.

Sample Letter to Administrator

Sample letter; please revise as necessary.

[Date]

Dear School Administrator:

[Name of district/agency contact] from the [district/agency] has arranged for [name of APERS-PE assessor] at [APERS assessor organization] to conduct an Autism Program Environment Rating Scale–Preschool/Elementary (APERS-PE) assessment at your school on [assessment date]. The APERS-PE is a comprehensive assessment of the quality of programs serving students with autism. The results of this assessment will be shared with the primary teacher of the autism program.

[Name of APERS-PE assessor] will visit with the teacher and observe activities that occur in their classroom and other classrooms in the school that provide services for [two/three] students with autism. We will also interview the primary teacher and other team members who work with one or more of the students in the classroom with autism, as well as the parent(s) of the student(s). We will obtain parent permission to interview the parents as part of this learning opportunity. [Name of district/agency contact] has arranged this activity with the primary classroom teacher in your school, and they are willing to participate in this learning activity. [Name of APERS-PE assessor] will observe the classroom(s), interview the teacher and other team members, and review the most recent IEP(s) for the selected student(s).

Our hope is that the time spent in the classroom and interviewing the teacher will benefit the classroom/program by the feedback we provide.

We appreciate the participation of your school in supporting this learning activity and wanted to inform you of the date and what you can expect. If you have questions, please either follow up with [Name of district/agency contact] or with me through the contact information below. Thank you.

Sincerely,

[Name and contact information of APERS-PE assessor]

APERS-PE Planning Guide (Preliminary Interview)

Activity	Participant			Location	Time
• Preliminary interview	Key school staff member Reminders: • Choose two to three target students • Obtain IEPs of two to three target students • Obtain class schedules/room numbers of two to three target students • Select person to support environmental scan • Schedule observations • Arrange to notify teachers about observation				
• Environmental scan	General: • Cafeteria • Library • Media Center • Other:	Student 1: • Primary class teacher/room number • Recess/PE • Specials	Student 2: • Primary class teacher/room number • Recess/PE • Specials	Student 3: • Primary class teacher/room number • Recess/PE • Specials	
• IEP reviews	Student 1				
	Student 2				
	Student 3				
• Observations	Notes for scheduling of student observations for two to three target students:				
• Initial scoring/ interview preparation	Notes about initial scoring/interview preparation:				

Activity	Participant	Location	Time
• Interviews	Special educator 1: (special educator for student in self-contained program) gaining access to alternate assessment		
	Special educator 2: (special educator for student in inclusive program—resource teacher)		
	General educator 1: (general educator for core academics for student in inclusive program)		
	General educator 2: (general educator—core or other who serves students in inclusive environments)		
	Administrator: (principal, assistant principal, special education coordinator)		
	Speech-language pathologist		
	Team member: (related services provider, other)		
	Parent: (parent of student in self-contained program)		
	Parent: (parent of student in inclusive environment)		
• Final scoring	Notes about final scoring:		

APERS PE   *Autism Program Environment Rating Scale-Preschool/Elementary (APERS-PE)* by Samuel L. Odom, Ann M. Sam, and Ann W. Cox. Copyright © 2024 by The University of North Carolina at Chapel Hill. All rights reserved. Published by Paul H. Brookes Publishing Co., Inc.

Sample Letter to Parent

Sample letter; please revise as necessary.

[Date]

Dear Parent:

I'm writing to you because your child's classroom is participating in an assessment of the quality of classrooms and programs that include students who have autism. The Autism Program Environment Rating Scale-Preschool/Elementary (APERS-PE) is a comprehensive assessment of the quality of programs serving students with autism, developed by the National Professional Development Center on Autism. The results of this assessment will be shared with the primary teacher of the separate program.

We will conduct the APERS-PE on [date]. We will gather information on the quality of the program through observations in the classroom, interviews, and reviewing relevant IEP information. Your child's teacher will receive information on the classrooms strengths and areas they may want to focus on for further improvement. We will provide the classroom teacher resources to get started on the areas the teacher sees as priorities.

As part of this process, we would like to gather interview information to make sure to get multiple perspectives on the classroom program. One very important perspective is that of parents.

Would you be available for a 45-minute or less interview over the phone on [date]? The interview is confidential. Your thoughts will not be shared directly with your child's teacher or other school staff. As part of our scoring process, we will incorporate your interview information with other interviews with your child's teacher and other team members. In addition, would you allow us to review your child's IEP and other reports in your child's file. Again, this information would only be seen by the APERS assessor and not shared with anyone else.

Thank you in advance for considering this request. Please let your child's teacher know if you are available and when. The teacher is making a schedule of the day and will best know when we will be available to speak with you. If you have questions you would like to address to me, you can reach me at [name/contact info of APERS-PE assessor].

We look forward to learning from and supporting your child's classroom. For more information on the National Professional Development Center on Autism, please visit http://autismpdc.fpg.unc.edu.

Sincerely,

[Name and contact information of APERS-PE assessor]

3 Scoring the APERS

"Researchers use a rating scale in research when they intend to associate a qualitative measure with the various aspects of a product or feature. Generally, this scale is used to evaluate the performance of a product or service, employee skills, customer service performances, processes followed for a particular goal, etc."
—Bhat (2019)

Practitioners and educators use the APERS to assess program quality the same way as researchers use a rating scale in their research. That is, teachers, administrators, or policy makers are interested in measuring how well the educational program (the service), teacher–student interactions (employee skills), family involvement (customer service performances), and instruction/curriculum (processes) are operating to meet the goal of providing a high-quality educational experience for students with autism. In this chapter, we describe procedures for using the information coders collect in their observations, interviews, and document analyses to rate individual items.

DATA USED TO SCORE THE APERS-PE

APERS-PE items are rated based on data from classroom observations and interviews with school staff and with parent(s) of the focal child(ren) observed, as well as document and, particularly, IEP review. As discussed in Chapter 2, the rater should be familiar with the items on the APERS-PE Scoring Tool before conducting the APERS, and previous training when possible is advised. The rater should also have the following guidance documents available while conducting the APERS-PE:

- APERS-PE Observer Guide: Things to Remember to Look For.

- APERS-PE Interview protocols

- APERS-PE Record Review Guide: Things to Remember to Look For

Listed domains in the Observer Guide and Record Review Guide correspond to the domains on the Scoring Tool, and Things to Remember to Look For are related to assessment items (see Figure 3.1). Questions on the interview protocols correspond to specific domains and items as noted on the protocols.

Classroom Observations

Classroom observations are essential for conducting the APERS. These observations provide the rater with important information on the quality of the classroom, including interactions staff have with students, families, and colleagues; learning, communication, and social opportunities for students; and how interfering behaviors are addressed in the setting.

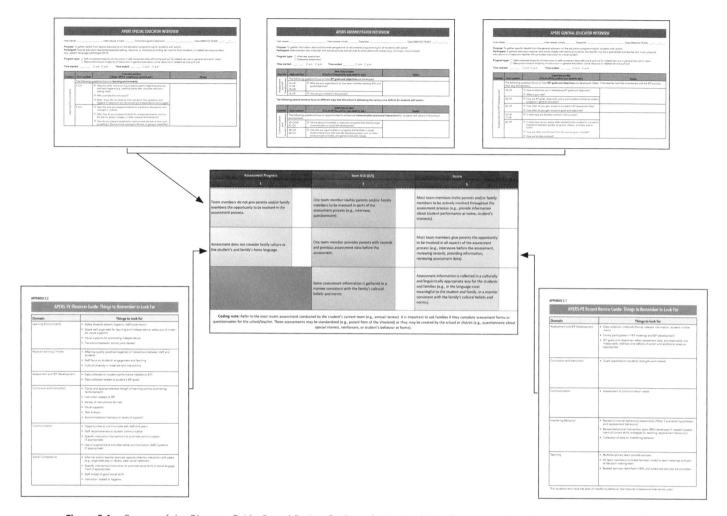

Figure 3.1. Content of the Observer Guide, Record Review Guide, and Interview Protocols corresponds to the domains and items in the Scoring Tool.

Interviews

Although the classroom observations are important and the primary source used when rating items, it is not possible for the rater to observe everything in a 3- to 6-hour period. The interviews are used to supplement the observations in order to rate items that are not easily observed (e.g., information on how decisions are made during IEP meetings, a social skills group not held during the observation period). If there is inconsistency among the observations, interview, and document review information, then priority should be given to the observational data.

Record Review

Record reviews are critical in order to gain an understanding of the educational needs and goals of the student, services and accommodations provided, as well as other contextual information. During the observation, it is critical to observe how these services and accommodations are implemented as well as how data are collected.

REVIEWING DATA

After conducting the observations, completing the interviews, and finishing the document review, the rater should read through all the data that have been collected. The rater should allocate 45–60 minutes for that review.

Although it is not optimal, sometimes data collection occurs over an extended period of time. For example, several interviews might not be able to be conducted until a couple of weeks after the observations, or teacher absences may extend the period of time when the observations can occur. Unfortunately, memory of events in school settings or interviews with staff often fade fast. Reviewing the notes from interviews or observations remind the reviewer of the data that was originally collected.

▨ Tips for Reviewing Data and Scoring

Score the APERS as soon as possible following your observation. Plan for about an hour to review your collected notes and data before scoring.

MAKING JUDGMENTS ABOUT APERS-PE ITEMS

Judgments about assessment items are by nature subjective—the raters use the information they have about the thing being rated (in our case quality of a school program) and make a judgment about the degree to which an item fits. As previously noted, raters have three sources of information from which to draw when making judgments about APERS-PE items: 1) observations, 2) interviews, and 3) records. Figure 3.2 presents a conceptual scheme for making these judgments. Also, Figure 3.3 indicates which type of information a rater would use to complete each item in the APERS-PE.

In some cases, the data overlap and confirm the rating to be provided. For example, the rater may observe a teacher using a standardized curriculum for promoting social skills, they also report using the curriculum in the interview, the parent comments on the materials the teacher sends home associated with the curriculum, and the curriculum content aligns with the goal and objectives on the IEP. In other cases, there may be only one source of information, but it confirms that a quality indicator is occurring (e.g., only the observations confirm the schedule and routines that are followed in the class). Data are consistent in both cases. The rater can compare the information gathered to the relevant items and indicators within the domains for Social Competence and Curriculum and Instruction.

Also, there may be cases in which conflicting information occurs (e.g., the teachers report one thing and the parents report another), in which case the rater will have to make a judgment based on their experiences in the program. As noted, the observational information should take priority over interviews. For example, the teacher may report during the interview that they take data on interfering behavior as behaviors occur frequently. Yet, during the observation, the rater does not observe any adults (teacher or paraprofessionals) collecting data on the interfering behavior when it occurs several times during the day. In this example, the rater would score based on what was observed, not what was noted during the interview because there were several opportunities to observe data collection. The rater may collect additional information, however. Using the previous example, the rater could ask the teacher to see the data they have collected on the interfering behavior (record review). If the collected data represents consistent data collection of the interfering behavior, then this additional information could be using when scoring.

▨ Tips for Interpreting Conflicting Information

Use your clinical judgement when you receive conflicting information, and, remember, observations always trump interviews.

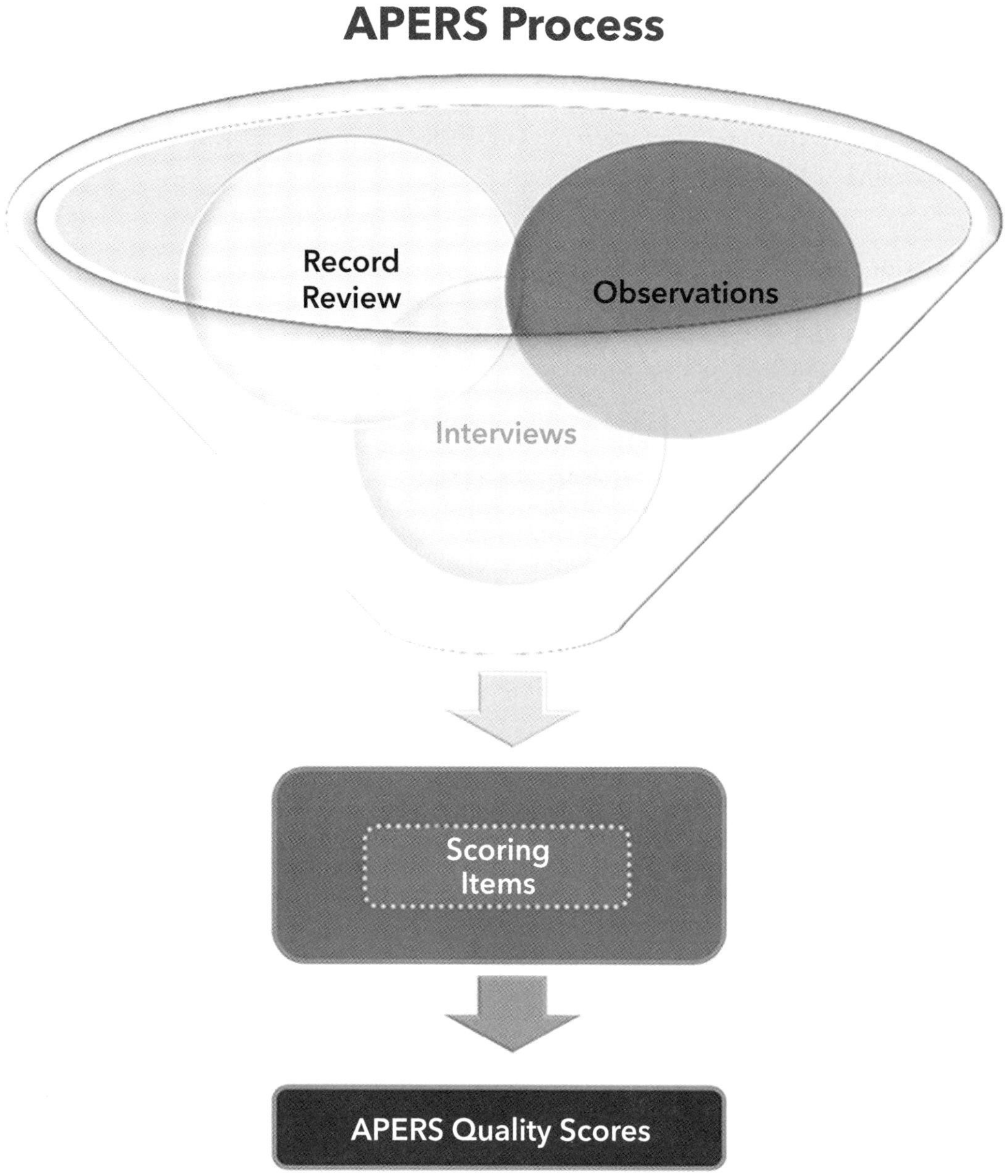

APERS Process

Figure 3.2. How the APERS distills ratings from observations, interviews, and document analysis.

USING THE SCORING TOOL

As previously noted, the content of guidance documents raters have on hand while administering the APERS corresponds to the domains, items, and indicators within the APERS Scoring Tool. This Scoring Tool is an Excel spreadsheet that serves multiple functions:

1. The rater reviews the indicators for each item in the spreadsheet. For each item, the rater determines which indicators best correspond to what the rater learned about the program through observation, interviews, and review of student records.

2. The rater marks those indicators for the item.

Item #	Dimension	Observation	Records	Interview
Learning Environments				
1	Safety			
2	Safety			
3	Safety			
4	Organization of Learning Environments			
5	Organization of Learning Environments			
6	Materials			
7	Materials			
8	Visual Schedules			
9	Transitions Within the School Day			
Positive Learning Climate				
10	Staff-Student Interactions			
11	Staff-Student Interactions			
12	Staff Behaviors			
13	Staff Behaviors			
14	Promoting Diversity			
Assessment and IEP Development				
15	Assessing Student Progress			
16	Assessment Process			
17	IEP Goals			
18	IEP Goals			
19	IEP Goals			
20	Program Transition Planning			
Curriculum and Instruction				
21	Instructional Format			
22	Instructional Content			
23	Instructional Strategies			
24	Instructional Strategies			
25	Instructional Content			
26	Instructional Format			
27	Instructional Strategies			
28	Instructional Strategies			
29	Instructional Strategies			
30	Instructional Strategies			
31	Instructional Strategies			
32	Instructional Strategies			

Figure 3.3. Data used to score items for APERS-PE.

(continued)

Figure 3.3. *(continued)*

Item #	Dimension	Observation	Records	Interview
Communication				
33	Planning for Communication			
34	Communication Rich Environment			
35	Individualized Communication Instruction			
36	Responsiveness to Student Communication			
37	Communication Systems			
Social Competence				
38	Arranging Opportunities			
39	Arranging Opportunities			
40	Teaching and Modeling			
41	Social Skills Instruction			
42	Peer Social Networks			
Personal Independence and Competence				
43	Personal Independence			
44	Personal Independence			
45	Personal Independence			
46	Self-Management			
Interfering Behavior				
47	Proactive Strategies			
48	Behavioral Assessment			
49	Behavioral Assessment			
50	Behavior Management			
51	Data Collection			
Family Involvement				
52	Building Rapport With Families			
53	Communication			
54	Communication			
55	Parent Teacher Meetings			
Teaming				
56	Team Training			
57	Team Membership			
58	Team Membership			
59	Team Membership			
60	Team Meetings			
61	Team Meetings			
62	Implementation			

3. The Scoring Tool automatically calculates a score for the item based on the indicators the rater has marked.

4. Based on the item scores, the Scoring Tool automatically calculates

   • A Total Domain Score for each domain (see Figure 3.4a)

   • A Subdomain Score for each dimension or subdomain within a particular domain (see Figure 3.4b)

These scores will appear in the tab labeled **Summary.**

5. Based on the Total Domain Scores and Subdomain Scores, the **Summary** tab of the Scoring Tool automatically generates bar graphs representing

   • A complete APERS profile by domain (see Figure 3.4c). On this graph, the vertical line at the left represents a 1 rating, the line in the middle represents a 3 rating, and the line at the right represent the 5 rating.

   • A snapshot of each of the 10 domains (see Figure 3.4d).

These graphs will appear in the tab labeled **Summary.**

a.

Domain	Score
1. Learning Environments	4.2
2. Positive Learning Climate	3.4
3. Assessment and IEP Development	2.5
4. Curriculum and Instruction	3.6
5. Communication	2.8
6. Social Competence	3.2
7. Personal Independence and Competence	3.8
8. Interfering Behavior	3.2
9. Family Involvement	4.0
10. Teaming	4.0
Overall	3.5

b.

Domain	Sub-domain	Score
Learning Environments	Safety	4.7
Learning Environments	Organization of Learning Environments	5.0
Learning Environments	Materials	4.0
Learning Environments	Visual Schedules	4.0
Learning Environments	Transitions Within the School Day	2.0
Positive Learning Climate	Staff-Student Interactions	4.0
Positive Learning Climate	Staff Behaviors	3.0
Positive Learning Climate	Promoting Diversity	3.0
Assessment and IEP Development	Assessing Student Progress	1.0
Assessment and IEP Development	Assessment Process	3.0
Assessment and IEP Development	IEP Goals	3.3
Assessment and IEP Development	Program Transition Planning	1.0

c.

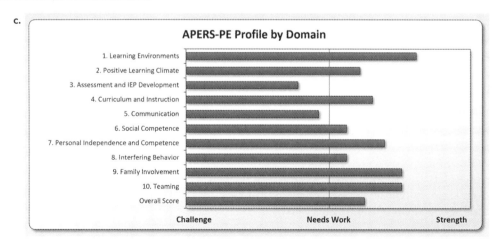

Figure 3.4. **a)** Total domain scores; **b)** total subdomain scores; **c)** APERS profile by domain; **d)** snapshot of each of the 10 domains.

(continued)

Figure 3.4. *(continued)*

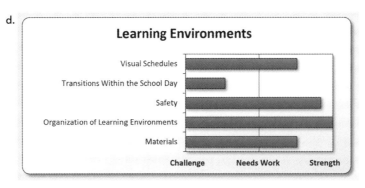

d.

IMPORTANT NOTE ABOUT THE SCORING TOOL: In order for the Scoring Tool to function correctly, macros must be enabled within the Excel file. Information on how to enable macros for this file can be found on the About the Downloads page.

ITEM FORMAT AND SCORING

The APERS employs a Likert-type rating scale consisting of five rating options. Ratings or scores for each item are generated by the Scoring Tool, an Excel spreadsheet. Based on the indicators the rater marks in the Scoring Tool, each item is automatically scored a 1, 2, 3, 4, or 5. An item score of 1 or 2 represents poor quality, an item score of 3 represents acceptable quality, and an item score of 4 or 5 represents high quality.

There are quality indicators for the 1, 3, and 5 ratings for each item in the Scoring Tool, which the rater judges as present or absent. The rater marks the indicators that are present based on what the rater observed and/or learned through interviews and review of student records (see Figure 3.5, a sample item from the Safety domain).

Note: If the program you are observing meets or exceeds the descriptions listed for a given item, then you must check all of the anchors in the "3" column for the item to score correctly. That is, if you check all of the anchors in the "5" column, then the item will not score a "5" until you also check all of the boxes in the "3" column.

SCORING DESCRIPTION BY DOMAINS

The APERS items are organized into domains that reflect the quality of a program. These domains are both conceptual and psychometric groupings (i.e., they align with the authors' conceptual framework of program features that reflect quality). They also have adequate within domain internal consistency as well as loading significantly on a central quality factor (see Chapter 6). In this section, each domain is described with clarification of any coding issues that may exist for individual items. Figure 3.3 provides information about which type of information to use for each item of the APERS-PE.

▨ Tips: APERS Domains

The APERS domains provide an overall description of quality of a program.

Learning Environments

The Learning Environments domain assesses the features of the classroom and school settings that support the learning and engagement of children and youth with autism. It could be thought of as the physical ecology of the class and school settings. The dimensions of the Learning Environments domain are Safety, Organization, Materials, Visual Schedules, and Transitions. Figure 3.5 provides an example Item 3 from the APERS-PE. The quality indicators range from unsanitary setting and no instruction related to hygiene at the 1 level to sanitary setting and instruction related to hygiene and hygienic skill independence at the 5 level. Also, some indicators for this item can be directly observed in the classroom, whereas the rater will have to draw on the interview with the teacher for other indicators because the item might not be able to be observed on the day of the observation.

Safety	Item #3 (O/I)	Score
1	3	5
The classroom/setting does not appear hygienic or sanitary (e.g., staff do not wash hands after helping students use the restroom, staff do not wash hands before handling food, materials appear dirty).	Sufficient hygiene and sanitation are maintained by team members in most activities.	Hygiene and sanitation are consistently maintained across activities.
No instruction is provided by team members to students regarding personal and basic hygiene (e.g., washing hands after using the restroom, wiping nose).	Some instruction is provided by one team member across activities about personal and basic hygiene (e.g., washing hands after using the restroom, wiping nose).	Basic and personal hygiene is part of classroom and/or community-based instruction (e.g., washing hands after using the restroom, wiping nose).
Team members do not encourage student independence during personal and basic hygiene tasks and activities (e.g., washing hands after using the restroom, wiping nose).	One team member encourages student independence during personal and basic hygiene tasks and activities (e.g., washing hands after using the restroom, wiping nose). The intent of Item 3 is that basic and personal hygiene are features of the program for all students as part of the school routine.	Most team members teach and encourage student independence during personal and basic hygiene tasks (e.g., washing hands after using the restroom, wiping nose).

Coding note: May not be applicable to older inclusive elementary programs. The intent of this item is that basic and personal hygiene are features of the entire educational program for all students as a part of the school routine. If instruction for Item 3 is not observed, supplement through interview.

Figure 3.5. Item 3 from the Learning Environments domain.

Positive Learning Climate

Positive Learning Climate assesses the degree to which the instruction and staff interactions are positive and nonpunitive in nature. It also includes an examination of the representation of diversity in curriculum materials. All of these items are collected through observations.

Staff Student Interactions		Item #11 (O)		Score	
1		3		5	
Team members often interact with students using a negative tone.		One team member's student interactions are positive, respectful, and warm (e.g., show respect for student's feelings, listen attentively, make eye contact).		Most team members in the classroom/setting engage students in positive, respectful, and warm interactions.	
Team members' interactions do not appear respectful of students' cultural or linguistic diversity.		One team member's student interactions appear respectful of students' cultural or linguistic diversity.		Most team members' interactions appear respectful of students' cultural or linguistic diversity.	

Figure 3.6. Item 11 from the Positive Learning Climate domain.

Figure 3.6 provides an example of Item 11 from the APERS-PE that focuses on the socially positive interactions that occur between teachers and students.

Assessment and IEP Development

Assessment is the basis on which individualized programs for students with autism should be planned. In this section, the rater evaluates the quality of the assessment process, the use of assessment to measure student progress, and the development of IEP goals. This domain also includes the degree to which programs include planning for students' transition between schools, as appropriate for students in preschool and elementary programs (APERS-PE). An example of Item 20 from this domain appears in Figure 3.7. Because it is unlikely that the rater will be able to observe the assessment process or IEP meetings, information for these items is drawn from interviews and record review (e.g., IEP, assessment records).

Program Transition Planning		Item #20 (R/I)		Score	
1		3		5	
Assessments do not include information related to transitions between grades, programs, or other transitions.		One team member develops some appropriate and measurable annual goals and services that support students' transition to next class.		Practitioner(s) from student's next educational program is invited to contribute to assessment and transition planning process.	
		Most team members make consistent efforts to involve families (e.g., soliciting ideas for goals, sharing draft goals, providing opportunities for feedback) in developing plans for transition when appropriate.		Assessment results are shared with students' next educational program.	

Figure 3.7. Item 20 from the Assessment and IEP Development domain.

Curriculum and Instruction

The items for the Curriculum and Instruction domain are designed to assess the teaching process and specific practices the school or program staff use to support students' learning and accomplishment of IEP goals. They address topics such as setting up the instructional session or experience, types of prompting used, use of visual supports during the lessons or learning sessions, sensory accommodations, opportunities to respond, and use of task analysis. The raters should be able to complete most of these items from their observations, but if instances were not observed in the program, then raters can ask the teacher or other staff about the instructional feature during the interview. Figure 3.8 contains an example of Item 28 from the Curriculum and Instruction domain from the APERS-PE.

Instruction Strategies	Item #28 (O/I)	Score
1	3	5
Team members do not use reinforcers to increase desired student performance.	One team member conducts a reinforcement assessment or uses a standard process to determine appropriate individual reinforcement.	Most team members use natural reinforcers (e.g., grades, reduction in homework, free time at end of class, access to preferred activity or object).
Team members use negative consequences in responding to errors during instruction (e.g., over-correction, humiliation).	One team member uses positive reinforcers more frequently than negative consequences.	Most team members apply positive reinforcers consistently and contingently to increase desired student performance.
	One team member applies positive reinforcers consistently and contingently to increase desired student performance.	Most team members use positive reinforcers more frequently than negative consequences.
Coding note: It is important the teachers have a process for determining reinforcers and can state it. Do not score if not applicable to inclusive program, use manual override.		

Figure 3.8. Item 28 from the Curriculum and Instruction domain.

Communication

Communication is a major challenge for students with autism. In fact, it is one of the defining features. As such, providing a strong emphasis on communication skills is an important feature of school programs for most students with autism. Items in this domain address richness of the communication environment, the planning process for intervention, individualized instruction that focuses on communication, responsiveness of teachers to students' communication, and, for some students, the use of an augmentative and alternative (AAC) communication system. Raters can draw from their observations to make judgments about most of these items, although, again, they may be supplemented by interviews. An example of Item 35 from the Communication domain appears in Figure 3.9.

Individualized Communication Instruction	Item #35 (O/R/I)	Score
1	3	5
Team members do not use consistent instructional strategies for promoting student communication (e.g., prompting, appropriate wait time, reinforcement).	One team member consistently uses instructional strategies to promote student communication development (e.g., prompting, appropriate wait time, reinforcement) in at least two environments (e.g., recess, lunch, classroom, therapy room).	Most team members consistently use instructional strategies to promote student communication development (e.g., prompting, appropriate wait time, reinforcement) across school and environments.
	One team member implements individualized systematic instruction which matches student needs as identified in the assessment (e.g., modeling the use of the communication system, teaching new vocabulary, role playing conversations) and emphasizes functional communication. (Do not select if no assessment was used. Impressionistic observation and notes in school do not count as data.)	Most team members implement individualized systematic instruction which matches student needs as identified in the assessment (e.g., modeling the use of the communication system, teaching new vocabulary, role playing conversations) and emphasizes functional and spontaneous communication, whereby the student has the opportunity to initiate communication without the need for prompting or cueing.

Figure 3.9. Item 35 from the Communication domain.

Social Competence

This domain assesses features of the program that support students' social interactions and relationships with peers. Like communication challenges, social challenges are a hallmark of autism. Dimensions of programs that reflect quality are arranging the environment to create opportunity for social interaction, teaching and modeling, and implementing peer social network activities. An example of Item 42 from the APERS-PE appears in Figure 3.10. The raters

Peer Social Networks		Item #42 (O/I)		Score	
1		**3**		**5**	
Peer social networks are not implemented as part of the school's core curriculum (e.g., school does not provide instruction to typically developing peers about how to be peer buddies).		Peer social network activities are implemented during at least two school-based activities (e.g., students with autism interact with typically developing peer buddies during lunch and during literacy instruction).		Formal peer social networks are part of the school's core curriculum (e.g., school provides instruction to typically developing peers about how to be peer buddies).	
				Three or more typically developing peers are identified to be peer buddies for students with autism across school and/or group activities (e.g., lunch, recess, PE, waiting for bus).	
Coding note: To score a 3, peer social networks can include school-wide peer buddies' programs, even if no specific training has been provided by the school. To score a 5, peer buddies have to be intentionally assigned to students with autism rather than peers assisting in classes only as a result of being classmates (the latter is covered under Item 41) and some training is provided to the peers. If the quality falls between the 1 and 3 anchors, score a 2.					

Figure 3.10. Item 42 from the Social Competence domain.

should be able to use their observations to make judgments about ratings in this domain; although they may supplement their observations with information from interviews.

Personal Independence and Competence

Students with autism sometimes become dependent on adults for prompting their engagement in instructions or activities of daily living. An important feature of programs for students with autism is to provide accommodations that support independent engagement, self-advocacy, and self-management. Both the preschool/elementary and middle/high school versions of the APERS include items that assess these features of the program environment. An example of Item 44 from the APERS-PE is included in Figure 3.11. Both observation and interview information will inform the rater's judgment about these items.

Personal Independence		Item #44 (O)		Score	
1		**3**		**5**	
Team members do not use any strategies to promote students' personal independence in routines and activities (e.g., picture schedules, transition objects, checklists, PDAs/personal organizers, assignment notebooks, binders, calendars, daily planners).		One team member uses at least two strategies to promote students' personal independence in routines and activities (e.g., picture schedules, transition objects, checklists, PDAs/personal organizers, assignment notebooks, binders, calendars, daily planners).		Most team members use three or more strategies across classroom activities to promote students' personal independence (e.g., picture schedules, transition objects, checklists, PDAs/personal organizers, assignment notebooks, binders, calendars, daily planners).	
When supporting students, team members consistently position themselves in very close proximity to students, eliminating opportunities for students to function independently.*		When supporting students, most team members position themselves far enough away to give students the opportunity to function independently but close enough to provide support when needed. Students who have significant physical disabilities or engage in violent or self-injurious behaviors may require a team member to constantly remain in close proximity. If this is the case, select item.		Most team members provide support as needed in social situations in a way that allows the student to interact directly with peers and school staff, refraining from being an intermediary or speaking for the student.	
When supporting students, team members position themselves at a distance from which they are unable to effectively provide support when needed.					
Coding note: *To score a 5, team members' facilitation of independence must occur across three or more activities and include social situations.					

Figure 3.11. Item 44 from the Personal Independence and Competence domain.

Interfering Behavior

Rigid and repetitive behaviors are another defining feature of autism. A feature of program quality is the degree to which staff can plan and carry out programs that address behaviors that interfere with and limit students' engagement in learning activities. The APERS-PE includes ratings of behavioral assessment, behavior management, and data collection. An example of

Behavioral Assessment		Item #49 (R/I)		Score	
1		3		5	
Team members do not develop an intervention plan to address interfering behaviors.		One team member (e.g., special education teacher, general education teacher, SLP) develops an intervention plan to address interfering behaviors when they occur.		Team members develop a comprehensive intervention plan in collaboration with family, which includes assessment of current skills and any interfering behaviors, instructional strategies for teaching replacement behaviors and a plan for what to do if interfering behavior continues to occur.	
		One team member implements identified strategies and interventions in a consistent manner when the interfering behaviors occur.		Most team members implement identified strategies and interventions in a consistent manner when the interfering behaviors occur to maintain implementation fidelity.	
Coding note: If no behaviors rise to level of interfering, score item as N/A.					

Figure 3.12. Item 49 from the Interfering Behavior domain.

Item 49 from this domain appears in Figure 3.12. For this domain, the rater may draw information from observations, interviews, and record reviews (i.e., IEPs, BIPs). For some programs, students with autism may not have behavior issues that rise to the level that a plan will be needed. In those cases, the rater may code NA for appropriate items.

Family Involvement

The relationship that exists between the school and family, as well as family members' active involvement in the students' program, is a key feature of special education programs in general, and especially programs for students with autism. Such involvement is fostered by family members becoming a part of the interdisciplinary team that plans the student's program, ongoing and routine communication with family members, and scheduled meetings between the students' teacher and family members. Items capturing these dimensions of quality appear in the APERS-PE. Figure 3.13 contains an example of Item 53 from this domain. In most cases, raters will have to depend on interviews with family members and the school staff to score these items.

Communication		Item #53 (I)		Score	
1		3		5	
Team members do not have regular communication with family.		One team member at least has a system for regular and frequent communication that is consistently used (e.g., email, primary contact person, monthly newsletter), but this may be identical for all families.		One team member has a system for regular communication that is individualized to each family (e.g., email, primary contact person, phone calls).	
In the IEP conference, team members frequently use technical terms and provide no explanation to families.		One team member avoids the use of jargon and acronyms when communicating with parents/families, or technical terms are explained when they must be used.		Most team members avoid jargon and acronyms when communicating with parents/families, or technical terms are explained when they must be used.	

Figure 3.13. Item 53 from the Family Involvement domain.

Teaming

Educational programs for students with autism are designed and implemented by interdisciplinary teams of professionals, which also include family members. The organization of the team and communication among team members are an important contribution to the overall quality of programs for students with autism. The Teaming domain includes items assessing team training, team membership, team meetings, and implementation. Raters draw information for making judgments about items in this domain from interviews with the special education teacher(s), general education teachers, related services providers such as SLPs, administrators, and family members. An example of Item 57 for this domain appears in Figure 3.14.

Team Membership	Item #57 (R/I)	Score
1	3	5
One team member makes decisions about students' instructional programs, without consultation with other team members or parents.	A multidisciplinary team, consisting of at least two practitioners (e.g., special education teacher, speech-language pathologist), makes decisions about students' instructional programs.	A multidisciplinary team that consists of all practitioners who provide services to students (e.g., teacher, speech-language pathologist, occupational therapist, psychologist, general educator), makes decisions about students' instructional programs.
Team members do not actively include (e.g., do not invite to meetings, do not ask for feedback) parents and students as equal members of the team.	Parents and students (if developmentally appropriate) are invited to become members of the team.	
	Team members actively include (e.g., invite to meetings, ask for feedback) parents and students as equal members of the team.	
Coding note: Confirm team membership from IEP records and Special Educator teacher interview and parent report.		

Figure 3.14. Item 57 from the Teaming domain.

AUTOMATIC GENERATION OF SCORES

An automated scoring system is built into the APERS-PE Scoring Tool. Within the Scoring Tool, raters mark the indicators that they judge as being present for an item. The program will automatically calculate a score for that item based on the indicators the rater has marked within each column.

Figure 3.15 summarizes how a score of 1, 2, 3, 4, or 5 is generated based on the combination of indicators the rater has marked. For any given item: If the rater has marked *any* of the indicators in the 1 column, then the program generates a score of 1. If the rater has not marked *any* indicators in the 1 column *and* has marked *at least one, but not all of,* the indicators in the 3 column, then the program generates a score of 2. If the rater has marked *all* of the indicators in the 3 column

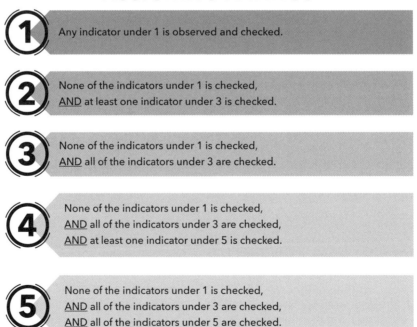

ASSIGNING RATINGS

1 Any indicator under 1 is observed and checked.

2 None of the indicators under 1 is checked,
AND at least one indicator under 3 is checked.

3 None of the indicators under 1 is checked,
AND all of the indicators under 3 are checked.

4 None of the indicators under 1 is checked,
AND all of the indicators under 3 are checked,
AND at least one indicator under 5 is checked.

5 None of the indicators under 1 is checked,
AND all of the indicators under 3 are checked,
AND all of the indicators under 5 are checked.

Figure 3.15. How item ratings are assigned.

and has not marked *any* of the indicators in the 1 column, then the program generates a score of 3. If the rater has marked *all* of the indicators in the 3 column and has marked *at least one, but not all of,* the indicators in the 5 column, then the program generates a score of 4. If the rater has marked all of the 3 *and* all of the 5 indicators for an item, then the program generates a score of 5.

Item Examples: Automatic Score Calculation

To illustrate how scores are calculated, Figures 3.16 and 3.17 show examples of two items—one scored from observation and one from interview. Each item has quality indicators organized in columns labeled 1, 3, and 5 as previously described.

Example 1   Figure 3.16 shows APERS-PE Item 5. This item is from the Learning Environments domain and focuses on the Organization of Learning Environments subdomain. The item assesses how well the physical structure and boundaries present in the learning environment support students' understanding of activities that take place in specific locations. It is scored based on the rater's observations of the environment.

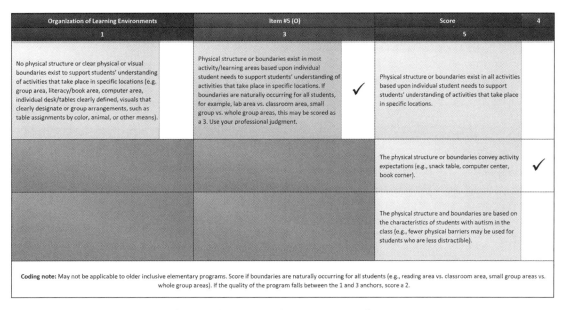

Figure 3.16.   Example 1: Sample item for which the Scoring Tool generates a score of 4.

For this item, the rater has not marked any indicators in the 1 column. The rater has marked one indicator in the 3 column to indicate that physical structure and boundaries supporting students' understanding of activities are present within most activities and learning areas in the environment. The rater has also marked one indicator in the 5 column to indicate that the structure and boundaries convey activity expectations.

Because the rater has marked *no* indicators in the 1 column, *all* indicators in the 3 column, and *at least one, but not all,* indicators in the 5 column, the Scoring Tool generated a score of 4 for this item.

Self-Management		Item #46 (O/I)		Score	2
1		3		5	
No strategies are used to promote self-management skills in students (e.g., helping students recognize their behavior by labeling it, helping students evaluate how they performed, including students in the reinforcement process, keeping track of assignments, keeping track of class grades).		Two or three strategies are used to promote self-management skills in students (e.g., helping students recognize their behavior by labeling it, helping students evaluate how they performed, including students in the reinforcement process, keeping track of assignments, keeping track of class grades).	✓	Four or more strategies are used to promote self-management skills in students (e.g., helping students recognize their behavior by labeling it, helping students evaluate how they performed, including students in the reinforcement process, keeping track of assignments, keeping track of class grades).	
		If appropriate, students are involved in the determination of self-management skills and strategies during team meetings.		If appropriate, students are involved in monitoring data for two or more IEP goals.	

Figure 3.17.   Example 2: Sample item for which the Scoring Tool generates a score of 2.

Example 2   Figure 3.17 shows APERS-PE Item 46. This item is from the Personal Independence and Competence domain and focuses on the Self-Management subdomain. The item assesses the extent to which the school staff use strategies to promote self-management in students, along with students' involvement in determining self-management skills and strategies and monitoring their own progress toward goals. It is scored based on the rater's interviews with the school staff.

For this item, the rater has not marked any indicators in the 1 column. The rater has marked one of the two indicators in the 3 column. Specifically, the rater has indicated that staff use two or three strategies to promote students' self-management but has not indicated that students are involved in determining self-management skills and strategies during team meetings. Finally, the rater has not marked any indicators in the 5 column.

Because the rater has marked *no* indicators in the 1 column, *at least one, but not all*, indicators in the 3 column, and *no* indicators in the 5 column, the Scoring Tool generated a score of 2 for this item.

Example 3   Figure 3.18 shows APERS-PE Item 11. This item is from the Positive Learning Climate domain and focuses on the Staff–Student Interactions subdomain. The item evaluates the interactions staff members have with students. The item focuses specifically on how positive interactions are and how respectful team members are to students' cultural and linguistic diversity.

Staff Student Interactions		Item #11 (O)		Score		1
1		**3**		**5**		
Team members often interact with students using a negative tone.	✓	One team member's student interactions are positive, respectful, and warm (e.g., show respect for student's feelings, listen attentively, make eye contact).		Most team members in the classroom/setting engage students in positive, respectful, and warm interactions.		
Team members' interactions do not appear respectful of students' cultural or linguistic diversity.		One team member's student interactions appear respectful of students' cultural or linguistic diversity.	✓	Most team members' interactions appear respectful of students' cultural or linguistic diversity.		

Figure 3.18.   Example 3: Sample item for which the Scoring Tool generates a score of 1.

For this item, the rater has marked that first indicator in column 1, noting that team members interactions are often negative in tone. In addition, the rater has marked one of the two indicators in the 3 column. Specifically, the rater has indicated one key team member is respectful of students' cultural or linguistic diversity. Finally, the rater has not marked any indicators in the 5 column.

Although the rater marked one indicator in the 3 column, the generated score is 1 because the rater has marked *one* indicator in the 1 column. Any indicators in the 1 column automatically generate a score of 1.

▨ Tips: APERS Domains

Scoring indicators in columns 3 and 5 will help with report writing, although the item will remain a score of 1.

Item Example: Use of Manual Override

There are special circumstances for a few items that require the rater to enter a manual override. The manual override is used under two circumstances:

1. When an item is not applicable to the school program being evaluated

2. When the 3 or 5 column for an item includes only one indicator, meaning that the scoring program cannot generate a score of 2 or 4

For example, students in a program such as an inclusive elementary school program may have no interfering behavior, so there is no need for the school staff to have completed an FBA. In such a case, the coder may enter an NA (not applicable) with the manual override.

For a small number of items, as noted, an item may include only one indicator in the 3 or 5 column. Item 42 of the APERS-PE Social Competence Domain is an example (see Figure 3.19). This item focuses on the Peer Social Networks subdomain. It assesses the extent to which the school staff implements peer social network activities as part of the core curriculum. It is scored based on the rater's interviews with the school staff.

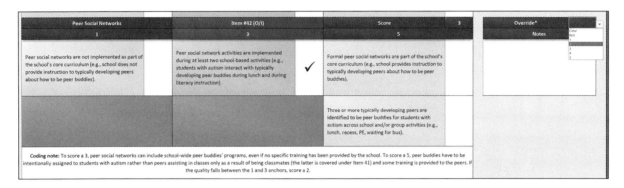

Figure 3.19. Sample item for which the rater uses manual override to assign a score of 2.

The scoring program does not allow a 2 code to automatically be generated because there is only one 3 indicator. In such situations, if the rater judges that the quality of the item, in this case social network activities, was below a 3 but above a 1, then the rater should activate the manual override and use the dropdown menu to enter a 2 rating. The rater would follow the same procedure if there were only one indicator for the 5 rating and the rater judges that the quality of the program was greater than the 3 but less than the single 5 indicator.

APERS-PE SCORING CALCULATOR

As previously noted, the APERS scoring program will automatically calculate total scores and scores for the APERS domains. These scores are reported as item ratings for individual items and average item ratings for domains and total score. To activate the program, the rater will need to fill in the identifying information on the "Program Assessment" tab. Then, the rater should code which indicators are present for each item, as judged from the data collected. When the rater has finished coding all items, they will click on the "Summary" tab, and the program will report mean item ratings for the total score, each domain, and each subdomain. If the coder has inadvertently not coded an item, "Incomplete" will show as the domain score, which will allow the rater to examine the domain and enter a code for the uncoded item(s).

An example of the summary scoring by domains and total score appears in Figure 3.20. The total score appears at the bottom. For this example, the overall quality is substantially above the 3 rating, indicated previously as a criterion level of medium quality. The Learning Environments, Personal Independence and Competence, and Family Involvement domains had scores of 4 or above, indicating that each of these was a strength for the program. The Assessment and IEP Development, Social Competence, and Interfering Behavior domains had scores below 3, indicating the lowest quality areas of the program, which the program staff should work to improve. In addition, Figure 3.20 shows "Incomplete" for the Curriculum and Instruction and Teaming domains, indicating that one or more items had not been coded for each of these specific domains.

Domain	Score
1. Learning Environments	4.6
2. Positive Learning Climate	3.6
3. Assessment and IEP Development	2.3
4. Curriculum and Instruction	Incomplete
5. Communication	4.2
6. Social Competence	2.6
7. Personal Independence and Competence	4.5
8. Interfering Behavior	2.6
9. Family Involvement	4.3
10. Teaming	Incomplete
Overall	Incomplete

Figure 3.20. Summary scores for the APERS-PE.

In addition, the APERS scoring program will generate a graph the data. An example of a graph for the data just presented appears in Figure 3.21. The overall score and domains are listed on the left, with the line next to the title indicating a 1 mean rating. The line in the middle of the graph indicates a 3 rating, and the vertical line to the right represents a 5. This graphic display allows the rater and program providers to quickly see the strengths and challenging quality areas in their program.

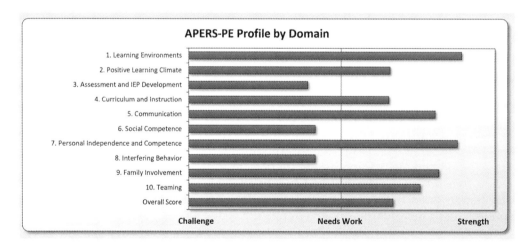

Figure 3.21. Graph of summary scores for the APERS-PE.

SUMMARY

In this chapter, we have provided specific information about scoring the APERS. Rating scales provide systematic but subjective judgments about a qualitative feature of, in our case, a program. They are designed for the rater to use all the sources of information available to them and judge the degree to which a feature of program quality is present. The procedures for gathering information (stated in Chapter 2) and specificity in describing indicators of quality to assist in assigning a rating are designed to promote an informed subjectivity that is reliable (which we discuss in our concluding chapter). In the next chapter, we discuss ways of using the information generated by the APERS to promote program quality. In Chapter 5, we will describe an abbreviated form of the APERS-PE, the APERS-PE/SA Tool, designed to provide formative feedback for teachers and other service providers in the school setting.

4 Using APERS Information

"Begin with the end in mind."
—Stephen Covey (2004)

The APERS-PE provides information about the quality of programs for children with autism that may be used to demonstrate or improve program quality. Leaders in local or statewide school systems may want to demonstrate to the community (e.g., board of education, legislative committees, parent or self-advocacy organizations) that the resources they are investing for autistic children and youth are resulting in high-quality programs. Parents may also want evidence that the programs in which their children are enrolled are of a high quality. Local program leaders may want information on which they can base plans for program improvement and professional development. Similarly, teachers and other service providers may want to evaluate their own efforts, identifying strengths and making plans for bolstering program features that are a challenge. Last, researchers may be interested in investigations of the effectiveness of programmatic approaches to improve quality.

Each of these groups may have different questions about program quality, as suggested by the exemplary questions in Table 4.1. The adage by Steven Covey (2004), "Begin with the end in mind," speaks well to the importance of identifying the purpose of assessing program quality and thinking ahead about how the information will be used. In this chapter, we discuss how APERS-PE information can be used for each of these purposes and provide examples of each.

NATIONAL, STATE, AND LOCAL LEADERS' USE OF APERS INFORMATION

Programs for autistic children and youth can be viewed from an ecological systems perspective. That is, the immediate school environments in which autistic students participate have direct influences on their learning and behavior, and the APERS assesses those features of the program environment that are likely to be influential. In his bioecological model, Bronfenbrenner would have called them the *microsystems* (Bronfenbrenner & Morris, 2006). There are microsystems other than the classroom in which students participate directly, such as the home, and also meetings of practitioners to share information and plan programing. These systems may influence the program environment (e.g., communication with the family), and when that happens, Bronfenbrenner called these the *mesosystem*. The APERS assesses these mesosystem influences as a feature of quality.

Table 4.1. Questions asked at different levels of the educational system

Levels of the educational system	Questions
National, state, and local policy makers	Does our investment result in high-quality programs?
District-level leaders	Are there professional development needs related to program quality?
School-level service providers	What are the areas of strengths in our program? Where do we need to improve?
Teachers and service providers	Are there ways that I can improve the quality of my classroom or school program?
Researchers	What school factors and teacher factors affect the quality of programs for autistic students?

Program environments are also influenced by factors that originate more distantly. Individual programs serving autistic children are influenced by factors at the national, state, and local policy makers' level. Policy makers are pushed to make sure their decisions about allocations of resources are made in reasonable and responsible manners. The Individuals with Disabilities Improvement Act (IDEIA) of 2004 (PL 108-446) dictates that students with disabilities receive a free appropriate public education (FAPE) that consists of scientifically proven practices (e.g., evidence-based practices). As noted in Chapter 1, the provision of such practices is based on, and reflected in, a foundation of program quality. The influence of the APERS would be as an information source in an ecological systems perspective. Policy makers in charge of allocating state resources then should be obligated and persuaded by information about the quality of the programs that their organization is delivering. The APERS may deliver such information by generating average quality ratings across programs, and even "finer-grained" information at the subdomain level. In sum, the role of education policy makers involves answering the question, "Does our investment result in high-quality programs?" and the related questions, "What is the overall quality of this particular program for students with autism?" and "How should finite resources be allocated to best support programs that serve these students well?" Information from the APERS can help them answer these questions, as described in the following examples.

How National Leaders Have Used APERS Results: OSEP Funding of the NPDC

One example of the use of such data occurred with the NPDC. The OSEP funded the NPDC to work with states to provide high-quality programs that incorporated evidence-based practices for autistic students. The center was initially funded for 2 years (2007–2009), with the provision that OSEP would provide additional funding for the next 3 years if evidence could be provided that it was accomplishing its mission. That is, federal decision makers were following Dr. James Gallagher's (2006) definition of public policy by making a decision about the allocation of scarce resources to an identified need. At the time, NPDC staff had worked with agencies in three states, collecting APERS data in programs at the beginning and end of the year. The APERS data revealed substantial increases in quality (i.e., higher mean item rating scores on APERS total and domain scores) for all three states. Table 4.2 lists the mean standardized effect sizes (i.e., Cohen's d) for changes from Fall to Spring of the school year. As a basis of comparison, in educational research, a Cohen's d effect size between .50 and .80 is considered moderate to high. Based on these data as well as positive effects on students' goal attainment, the decision makers at OSEP funded the center for 3 more years (2009–2012).

How State and Local Leaders Have Used APERS Results: State Adoptions of the NPDC Model

A second example was related to how the NPDC communicated with decision makers at the state and local program levels of the education system about the adoption of the NPDC model. In the subsequent 3 years of the NPDC, the center worked with nine programs. The NPDC

Table 4.2. Effect sizes for change in program quality across an academic year on APERS

Mean effect size by state		Mean effect size by grade level	
State	*Effect size*	*Grade level*	*Effect size*
Indiana	0.67	Preschool/elementary	0.75
Wisconsin	0.50	Middle/high	0.62
New Mexico	0.82		

reached out to state-level leadership (e.g., state-level departments of education), described the NPDC program, and shared the APERS data about changes in program quality, as well as other data (e.g., social validity data from teachers and schools). State leaders would then have to make a decision to submit an application to work with NPDC. The commitment involved allocating resources from their state for professional development, partnering with the NPDC team for training, and maintaining the partnership for a 2-year period. The positive findings about increases in program quality, generated by the APERS, was one influencing factor in attracting state departments to join in the partnership.

When a state was accepted as an NPDC state, the center staff then took the next step of sharing information, including APERS results, with local program leaders for them to make decisions about adopting the NPDC model in their program. Such decisions at the local level also require some allocation of resources, which literally reflects local buy-in. Implementation science tells us that such buy-in is essential for the successful adoption of program innovation (Odom et al., 2020).

How District Leaders Can Use APERS Results: Decision Making and Documenting Quality

District-level leaders are tasked with answering the question, "Are there professional development needs related to program quality?" They can use APERS information to help them answer this question and determine how best to allocate resources and which areas to target for professional development. They can also use APERS information to document program quality as it relates to the program's providing a FAPE for autistic students and providing instruction related to individual students' IEP goals. This is important information for family members and the community.

Making Decisions About Resources and Professional Development Leaders in school districts (e.g., assistant superintendents, coordinators of special education services) may also need and use information about autism program quality to make decisions about allocating resources. For example, information from the APERS may indicate that there are features of the school building environment that are unsafe or that the school may need to invest in evidence-based curriculum materials in a certain domain. The increased prevalence of autism in the general population (1 in 36 as of this writing) (Maenner et al., 2023) can be seen in the corollary increases in autistic students' eligibility for special education services as reported by OSEP (U.S. Department of Education, 2022; see Figure 4.1). In a moderate-size school district with 9,000 students (Hance, 2020), this would mean that approximately 250 students would be identified as autistic; in an elementary school of 600 students, there might be approximately 17 students with autism. Leaders who are responsible for special education programs are now confronted with a serious challenge related to teaching staff. Many staff in their district (e.g., principals, teachers, paraprofessionals) have not been trained to provide a high-quality program that meets the unique needs of this autistic student population.

Information from the APERS-PE could inform district leadership about quality of their current programs for autistic students and, if necessary, the need to improve quality. Such quality

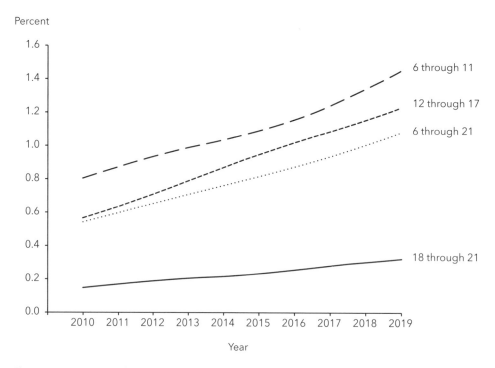

Figure 4.1. Increases in the percentage of autistic students eligible for special education services as reported from the OSEP 43rd Report to Congress on IDEA. (*Source:* U.S. Department of Education, Office of Special Education and Rehabilitative Services, Office of Special Education Programs, 2022.)

improvement is often accomplished through professional development. School district leaders building a professional development program that provides targeted training could use information from the APERS to guide their decisions about the content and form of training that would need to be offered. For example, a school district leader could identify five schools that are representative of their district and have the APERS completed in each school. The average APERS ratings might generate a profile such as the one in Figure 4.2. The vertical line in the center of this graph represents a mean "3" score, which reflects acceptable but not high quality. The data reflect strengths in Learning Environments, Family Involvement, and Teaming, with adequate quality in Positive Learning Climate, whereas there appear to be substantial challenges related to the assessment and curricular parts of the program, especially in the key areas of Communication, Social Competence, and Interfering Behavior. From these data, the district leader may decide to focus professional development on key areas of need, rather than providing a broader, general training about autism and its characteristics; although that should be a smaller part of the training.

Documenting Program Quality Related to FAPE and IEPs   The school system's obligation to provide a FAPE, as specified by IDEIA, is a second reason that school system leaders may wish to collect information about the quality of a program for autistic students. We propose that one necessary feature of appropriateness is that the program have at least adequate quality, which we define at a rating of "3" for the total score and domains. As part of IDEIA, parents have the right to advocate for their children's educational services, which can lead to due process hearings. Recent court rulings have further specified the definition of FAPE and how it is tied to the link between children's IEPs and features of the educational program provided (Yell, 2019). School leaders can provide APERS assessment findings to document the quality of a program provided to their students. Conversely, parents can use APERS to understand the features of a special education program that would be the essential foundation on which the school system would provide instruction related to their child's IEP.

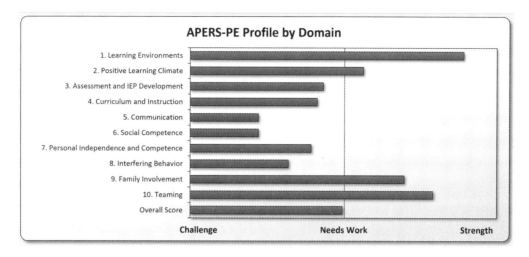

Figure 4.2. APERS-PE profile for school district.

How Building-Level Leaders Can Use APERS Results: Determining and Communicating About Areas for Improvement

Building-level leaders may be individuals who are part of the administration, such as principals or assistant principals, special education teachers, general education teachers, or related services providers. Leaders at this level can use APERS information to help them answer the questions, "What are the areas of strength in our programs or school?" "What are the areas in which we need to improve?"

When we worked with schools in our most recent projects described in Chapter 6 (Hume et al., 2022; Sam et al., 2021), we started by asking the school to organize an Autism Team consisting of individuals in the roles just mentioned. Our research coaches would conduct the APERS, although this assessment could also be conducted by the leader of the Autism Team or another individual in the school or district. The APERS would generate a graphic profile that displays the results, and then we would prepare a report. We recommend that the report

- Document strengths of the program

- Identify areas in which program quality could be improved

- Provide suggestions for program improvement

An example of such a report appears in the chapter appendix. This report is provided to the Autism Team in a debrief session that focuses on providing an overview of the strengths of the program in order for the Autism Team to continue to build on these successes. Next, three areas of growth are identified in the report and debrief session that should reflect key areas of need in the classroom and/or areas that could be easily addressed to increase buy-in at the school level. Specific suggestions for program improvement are presented to the team with links to resources (e.g., the AFIRM web site). Last, the Autism Team is encouraged to develop an action plan based on the report for addressing areas for improvement.

In the report example provided in the appendix, the APERS-PE was conducted in an elementary school that had both an inclusive (identified as general education) and self-contained (identified as separated) program for autistic students. The report includes APERS-PE profiles for each program. Strengths of the programs were Positive Learning Climate and Curriculum and Instruction for both programs. Areas of growth for the special education program were Social Competence and Learning Environments. Areas of growth for the inclusive program were Communication and Teaming. Also, the report reflects the qualitative difference between the two programs. In this case, the inclusive program had a generally higher quality, and the special education program had more areas for improvement. In this report, we provide a School Plan form in which Autism Team members and other school staff indicate areas of growth (improvement) they will address as a team, specific changes targeted, next steps, and a time line for accomplishments. We recommend that the Autism Team members and perhaps other school staff review the plan periodically (e.g., once a month) to identify the progress that has been made toward quality improvement.

How Teachers and Related Services Providers Can Use APERS Results: Improving Program Quality

Teachers in a special education classroom or who provide services through an inclusive program in a school might use APERS information for self-improvement of their program. This can be done through use of the full APERS assessment. If, however, they do not have the time and/or training to complete the full APERS, then staff members may use the APERS self-assessments as a tool for program improvement; these assessments are described in Chapter 5. In either case, educators may answer the question, "Are there ways I can improve quality of my classroom or school program?"

RESEARCH USES OF APERS RESULTS

Researchers may also use the APERS to address research questions related to program quality, and we provide examples of such research in Chapter 6. For example, researchers may be interested in the general quality of programs for autistic students and if certain quality dimensions are relatively stronger or weaker than others. Also, one could think of the APERS as a dependent variable that measures the effects of a comprehensive treatment program on program quality in a school or school systems. Examples of such research are described in Chapter 6.

SUMMARY

In this chapter, we have examined ways in which information generated by the APERS could be used by individuals who have different roles in the special educational system and would be using the information for different purposes. We employed an ecological system perspective in organizing this information, anticipating that policy makers and district administrators would have interests in and uses of the information that would differ from those of principals, supervisors, teachers, and service providers.

Chapters 1–4 have provided guidance on how to use the APERS-PE to assess and improve program quality. In the next chapter, we describe in detail how teachers and service providers may complete the APER-PE/SA and use the self-assessment results to improve program quality, identify areas for individual professional growth, and communicate with families about the program.

Sample Report

*Autism Program Evaluation Rating
Scale-Preschool/Elementary (APERS-PE) Debrief*

Reminder about the APERS process:
- Observed for one full school day
- Interviewed seven people across different roles
- Reviewed three IEPs

SETTING 1: Separate Setting (*Note:* This assessment is based on observations in a separate education setting at the school. Observations were in the classroom, in specials, in the hallways, and at lunch.)

AREAS OF STRENGTH

Positive Learning Climate

- *Example items:* Positive interactions with students; acknowledging efforts both informally and formally

- *Strengths noted:* Most team member interactions are warm, friendly, and respectful in the classrooms and in the hallways; student effort is acknowledged in a variety of ways both formally and informally (e.g., verbal praise, students encouraged to cheer for each other, high-fives, Golden Tickets); as an International Baccalaureate (IB) school, the school celebrates cultural diversity in all classrooms and throughout the school (evident in wall hangings and books in other languages, incorporated into instruction in the music room)

Curriculum and Instruction

- *Example items:* Visual supports used during instruction; opportunities for student participation; variety of instructional formats

- *Strengths noted:* Team members use a variety of instructional formats (whole group, small group, 1:1) and tailor instruction to students' understanding; instructions are provided in multiple ways to meet students' comprehension level; clear process is in place for generalizing skills from 1:1 instruction to group setting, then to outside of the classroom; academic and preacademic skills are addressed in a separate classroom, and instruction and support matches student need

AREAS FOR GROWTH

Social Competence

- *Example items:* Opportunities for peer social interactions; peer networks; modeling of social skills

- *Strengths noted:* Team members model good social skills; some opportunity for choice making are provided in the classrooms; some informal opportunities are provided for students to have social interaction with peers (sharing materials during whole-group instruction; lunch and recess take place with general education students).

- *Potential target areas:* Consider implementing formal support around social interactions in the classroom and across settings in the school; formal peer networks (providing instruction to typically developing peers to increase their understanding of social interactions with students with autism) are an effective way to provide support to students; consider, for example, peer buddies at lunch or recess or reading buddies during literacy instruction.

Learning Environments

- *Example items:* Use of classroom spaces; students have their own spaces; sufficient materials; overall schedule and written instructions

- *Strengths noted:* Some instruction is provided around personal hygiene activities; students have personal space to store their belongings; classroom space is sufficient and not overcrowded; sufficient materials are provided for all students to participate in planned activities

- *Potential target areas:* Some classroom items are broken or in disrepair; consider labeling classroom spaces (personal student spaces, seating, tables/stations) in developmentally appropriate manner for all students; students could benefit from the use of individualized daily schedules to promote understanding of routines and expectations in the classroom (From Autism Focused Intervention Resources & Modules [AFIRM], the module on Visual Supports—Schedules can be a useful resource for information on creating meaningful schedules for students.)

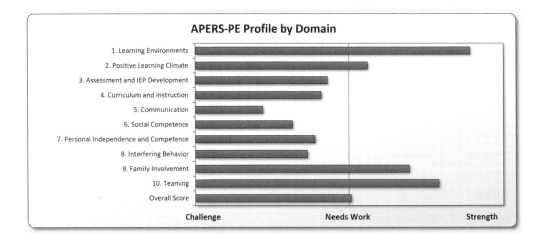

SETTING 2: General Education (*Note:* This assessment included observation of two students in their general education classrooms, during instruction in the resource room, during specials, and at lunch and recess.)

AREAS OF STRENGTH

Positive Learning Climate

- *Example items:* Positive interactions with students; acknowledging efforts both informally and formally

- *Strengths noted:* Key team members acknowledge students' efforts in a variety of ways, both formally (Golden Tickets, points earned) and informally (verbal praise, high-fives); team members greet and acknowledge students on arrival/departure and frequently in hallways; team members have positive and warm interactions with students; as an IB school, the school acknowledges and celebrates cultural diversity across many settings (evident in wall hangings and books, incorporated into instruction in the music and Spanish rooms, spotlight on other cultures in various classrooms)

Curriculum and Instruction

- *Example items:* Visual supports used during instruction; opportunities for student participation; variety of instructional formats

- *Strengths noted:* Team members use a variety of instructional formats across classrooms; opportunities for IEP goals to be addressed are provided across settings; preacademic and academic skills are addressed by team members; variety of reinforcements are in place across settings; students are given opportunities to respond to instruction and team members provide feedback appropriately

AREAS FOR GROWTH

Teaming

- *Example items:* Expertise in autism in team members; frequent opportunities for collaboration and communication

- *Strengths noted:* A multidisciplinary team is in place to make programming decisions for students; families are active members of the team and are involved in decision making.

- *Potential target areas:* Look for professional development opportunities for team members and school staff that target strategies for working with students with autism; inform all team members of student's programming for consistent implementation (e.g., share BIPs with specialists so strategies can be carried out across all school settings)

Communication

- *Example items:* Creating an environment that promotes need for communication and promoting communication across student's day

- *Strengths noted:* Frequent opportunities provided for partner talk across classroom settings; team members and school staff respond to students' communication attempts

- *Potential target areas:* Implement the use of instructional strategies to consistently promote communication across settings and team members; implement communication systems for students needing support with expressive communication; provide opportunities for students with stronger verbal skills and frequent opportunities to interact with typical peers; using scripts (written or visual) provides helpful cues to support their response to peers (e.g., a script that reminds student of what to say to a peer such as, "Your turn" or "It is my turn," a script that supports the student to respond to peers or adults when greeted)

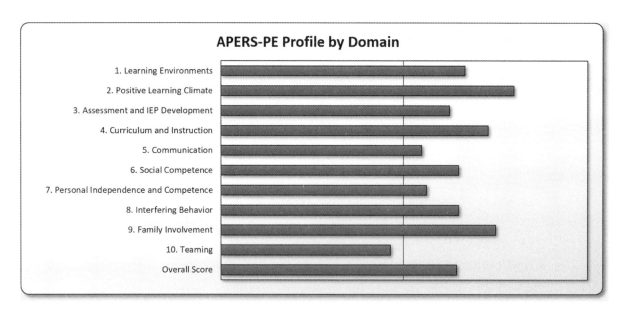

APERS SCHOOLWIDE OVERLAP

Across the school, the following strengths and potential areas for growth were noted related to the education of students with autism. The following are areas of overlap across the school.

AREAS OF STRENGTH

Positive Learning Climate

- Formal and informal acknowledgement of student efforts are frequently seen across the school program.
- Cultural diversity is celebrated across the school environment and incorporated into instruction, projects, posters, texts, and activities across classrooms and programs.
- Staff interact with students in a warm, friendly, and respectful way.

Curriculum and Instruction

- A variety of instructional formats are in place across classrooms; students have the opportunity to participate in whole-group, small-group, partner, and 1:1 instruction throughout their day.
- Students are given multiple opportunities to respond to instruction, and team members give feedback accordingly.
- Students' interests are considered (and even asked for) when planning instruction, rewards, and break activities.
- Task analysis is used to break complex skills down into manageable steps for students.
- Teachers are mindful of opportunities and strategies to support generalization of skills.

AREAS FOR GROWTH

Personal Independence and Competence

- *Strengths noted:* Some evidence of individualized schedules in place; direct instruction on self-advocacy across the school environment (e.g., teaching students to say no if something bothers them, encouraging students to discuss and work through difficulties with each other)

- *Potential target areas:*

  - Increase the use of visual supports for addressing the organization and completion of activities and assignments more independently (e.g., individual portable schedules that are developmentally appropriate, step-by-step instructions, organizational checklists). Visual supports can also reduce the number of prompts and verbal reminders needed from adults.

  - Support students in learning how to ask for help when needed and incorporate more opportunities for choice making throughout the day and across settings.

  - Increase the use of self-management strategies including supporting students in understanding their progress toward goals. These self-monitoring strategies are appropriate for students in both general education and separate settings.

Communication

- *Strengths noted:* Team members use instructional strategies that promote communication (e.g., waiting for a response, variety of prompting, verbal praise, opportunities for partner talk); team members are responsive to students' attempts to communicate

- *Potential target areas:*

  - Implement formal supports for expressive communication consistently and across school settings.

  - Individualize communication systems based on assessment of student strengths and needs.

  - Take advantage of student communication attempts by shaping or expanding their responses.

  - Visual supports, technology-aided instruction, scripts, modeling, and Picture Exchange Communication System (PECS) are effective evidence-based practices that can be used to support communication. See the AFIRM modules for further information on each practice.

APERS SCHOOL PLAN

Planning for next steps			
Growth area	Potential target areas	Next steps	Time line/ accomplishment

Planning for next steps			
Growth area	Potential target areas	Next steps	Time line/ accomplishment

5 APERS Self-Assessment

"Humble persons realize that they do not know everything and demonstrate the ability to inspect their own behavior . . . in order to prompt growth."
—Kilroy J. Oldster (2016)

The APERS-PE is a comprehensive assessment of the quality of educational programs for preschool and elementary school students with autism. As noted in previous chapters, raters who may not be members of the program staff observe in, and gather information from, programs to inform their ratings, and the information may be used for different purposes. The APERS-PE/SA has been developed for a different purpose and has a different format. The self-assessment is designed to be completed by program staff who have experience with and knowledge about the program. The explicit purpose is to provide program staff with a tool for reflection about their own practices, a forum for members of the staff to share and discuss the self-ratings with other staff members, and a valuable source of information for those who want to work on self-improvement of program quality in their classroom or program.

A note of caution here: the self-assessment is designed to generate formative information for program improvement. In most cases, the self-assessment can be completed more quickly than the full APERS-PE because it has fewer items and depends on the teacher or staff members' immediate familiarity with the program (therefore, observations, interviews, and record reviews do not have to be completed). We have purposely not assigned numerical scores to the instrument, but rather encourage teachers and other practitioners to look at patterns of responses (e.g., domains in which the ratings fall into the "challenge in our program" category). This information (possibly in combination with a report from an outside observer using the complete APERS-PE environmental assessment) enables teachers and others (e.g., coaches, technical assistance providers, district administrators) to gather information about program quality and develop a focused plan for program improvement.

The Self-Assessment Is Not a Substitute for the Full APERS

Because it does take less time to complete, raters might be tempted to use the self-assessment version rather than the full APERS-PE when evaluating an entire program. In such cases, the self-assessment is being used for a purpose other than that for which it was designed and should not be interpreted as APERS-PE assessment scores.

The following sections describe the item format and domains for the APERS-PE/SA, procedures for completing it, and how to use this information to improve program quality.

FORMAT FOR ITEMS

As can be seen on the APERS-PE/SA sample item provided next, the items are organized into three classifications based on the quality of the practice:

1. "This is a challenge in our program."

2. "This element is consistently in place, but we still have some work to do."

3. "This is a real strength in our program."

A description of features of the program is located under each rating category, and the rater selects the category that best describes their program. More specific directions for completing the rating appear at the end of this chapter.

DESCRIPTION OF PROGRAM QUALITY DOMAINS

As with the full APERS-PE, the APERS-PE/SA tool is organized by 10 domains that assess program quality. Table 5.1 displays the organization by domains for each assessment. Thus, by assessing the degree to which these domains are addressed, teachers and staff can self-identify strengths and challenges within their classrooms. They could then use the information to promote the quality of their programs through professional development. An abbreviated description of each of the program quality domains follows with a few examples from the self-assessment tool. (Refer to the domain descriptions provided in previous chapters for the full APERS-PE assessment for a more in-depth discussion of program quality domains.)

Table 5.1. APERS-PE/SA items organized by domains

APERS-PE/SA	
Learning Environments	1–5
Positive Learning Climate	6–8
Assessment and IEP Development	9–11
Curriculum and Instruction	12–17
Communication	18–20
Social Competence	21–23
Personal Independence and Competence	24–25
Interfering Behavior	26–28
Family Involvement	29–30
Teaming	31–32

Learning Environments

The Learning Environments domain reflects the organization of the classroom and school settings in a way that promotes learning and includes such basic features as physical safety, physical arrangement of the class, schedules, and planning for transitions. These features of the classroom or program provide the foundation for implementing other learning activities. Figure 5.1 shows an example of an item that focuses on schedules.

Item #4		
This is a challenge in our program.	This element is consistently in place, but we still have some work to do.	This is a real strength in our program.
Schedules and/or written instructions (e.g., classroom assignments, written reminders) are not posted in the classroom. No individual visual schedules are used to support student transitions.	Limited schedules and/or written instructions (e.g., classroom assignments, written reminders) are present in the classroom. Two or more students have portable schedules (e.g., assignment notebook, planner, daily schedule) to support transitions.	Most team members provide and use schedules and/or written instructions in a variety of formats (e.g., picture, written) when necessary. Most students have portable schedules (e.g., assignment notebook, planner, daily schedule) to support transitions.

Figure 5.1. Item 4 from APERS-PE/SA addressing the program's use of schedules/written instructions.

Positive Learning Climate

The Positive Learning Climate domain assesses the degree to which the instruction and staff interactions are positive and nonpunitive in nature. It also includes how staff positively acknowledge students' effort (see Figure 5.2).

Item #7		
This is a challenge in our program.	This element is consistently in place, but we still have some work to do.	This is a real strength in our program.
Team members do not acknowledge students' efforts and positive behaviors.	One team member consistently acknowledges students' efforts and uses effective approaches to do so informally (e.g., pats on back, high fives) and/or formally (e.g., homework pass, soda, rewards, graded materials).	Most team members consistently acknowledge students' efforts in an individualized way, both informally (e.g., pats on the back, high fives) AND formally (e.g., notes, rewards, graded materials).

Figure 5.2. Item 7 from APERS-PE/SA addressing team member–student interactions within the program.

Assessment and IEP Development

Assessment is the cornerstone for the development of IEPs for students with autism. This domain includes items that assess the families' participation in the process, the process of assessment, and the use of assessment information to develop and monitor IEP goals. An example of an item from this domain is provided in Figure 5.3.

Item #11		
This is a challenge in our program.	This element is consistently in place, but we still have some work to do.	This is a real strength in our program.
Assessments do not include information related to transitions between grades, programs, or other transitions.	One team member develops goals related to transition from the assessment information and makes consistent efforts to involve families in assessment and transition planning.	Most team members participate in comprehensive assessments for transition that drive program plans, involve staff from next setting to contribute to planning process, and make consistent efforts to involve families in assessment and transition planning.

Figure 5.3. Item 11 from APERS-PE/SA addressing how assessments include information related to transitions between grades and programs.

Curriculum and Instruction

The items for the Curriculum and Instruction domain assess the general teaching process. Features of this process include the length of a lesson, visual supports provided, types of prompts provided, alternatives for responding, and plans for generalization. An example of an item from this domain is provided in Figure 5.4. The focus of this item is on the use of the instructional strategy of visual supports.

Item #16		
This is a challenge in our program.	**This element is consistently in place, but we still have some work to do.**	**This is a real strength in our program.**
Limited visual supports are used during instruction (e.g., outlines or notes for class period, teacher instructions for assignments written on the board, PowerPoint during lectures, "First, then," timers, scripts, picture instructions, iPad, iPod).	Visual supports are available and are sometimes used by one team member during instruction (e.g., outlines or notes for class period, instructions for assignments written on the board, PowerPoint during lectures, "First, then," timers, scripts, picture instructions, iPad, iPod).	Visual supports are routinely used by most team members and are individualized and available across settings and activities (e.g., outlines for class period, instructions for assignments written on the board, PowerPoint during lectures, timers, "First, then," timers, scripts, picture instructions, iPad, iPod).

Figure 5.4. Item 16 from APERS-PE/SA addressing use of visual supports in instruction.

Communication

Communication is a central part of this program for most students with autism. This domain includes items that assess opportunities students have for communication during the day, implementing specific instructional strategies that promote communication, and, for some students, the use of communication systems. Figure 5.5 provides an example of an item that addresses arranging the communication environment.

Item #18		
This is a challenge in our program.	**This element is consistently in place, but we still have some work to do.**	**This is a real strength in our program.**
Team members do not use strategies (e.g., environmental arrangement) to encourage student communication (e.g., students do not need to ask for items/materials to complete activities, environment is never altered/modified to encourage students to ask questions or comment).	One team member arranges environment to encourage students to communicate (e.g., materials are placed just out of reach so student needs to ask for them, student must ask a peer for a calculator or notebook); creates consistent, predictable routines; manipulates established routines to promote communication (e.g., pausing or changing the routine); and creates opportunities within classroom activities for students to respond or initiate communication.	In addition to arranging the environment to encourage students to communicate and creating opportunities within classroom activities for students to respond or initiate communication, most team members create opportunities for students to communicate with multiple partners (e.g., school staff, peers, community members) across multiple settings.

Figure 5.5. Item 18 from APERS-PE/SA addressing how team members arrange the communication environment.

Social Competence

Like communication, social skills are areas of need for most students with autism, and instructional programs that specifically support the development of social competence are critical. For the APERS-PE/SA, dimensions of programs that reflect quality include arranging the environment to create opportunity for social interaction, employing a specific instructional or intervention program to promote social skills, and implementing peer social network activities. The sample item in Figure 5.6 addresses peer social networks.

Item #23		
This is a challenge in our program.	This element is consistently in place, but we still have some work to do.	This is a real strength in our program.
Peer social networks are not implemented as part of the school's core curriculum (e.g., school does not provide instruction to typically developing peers about how to be peer buddies).	Formal peer social network activities are implemented during at least two school-based activities (e.g., students with autism interact with typically developing peer buddies during lunch and during literacy instruction).	Formal peer social networks are part of the school's core curriculum (e.g., school provides instruction to typically developing peers about how to be peer buddies), and three or more typically developing peers are identified to be peer buddies for students with autism across school- and/or community-based settings and activities (e.g., lunch, recess, going to football games, sitting in class, walking down hall).

Figure 5.6. Item 23 from APERS-PE/SA addressing peer social networks within the curriculum.

Personal Independence and Competence

Students with autism often do not initiate engagement in learning activities without prompts from teachers and may not be independent of teacher supports during other times of the school day. Items in this domain assess the degree to which teachers use strategies that directly promote independence during classrooms and school routines and also that promote self-management. An example of an item from the domain appears in Figure 5.7.

Item #24		
This is a challenge in our program.	This element is consistently in place, but we still have some work to do.	This is a real strength in our program.
No strategies are used to promote students' personal independence in routines and activities (e.g., picture schedules, transition objects, checklists, print or digital personal organizers, assignment notebooks, binders, calendars, daily planners).	One team member uses at least two strategies to promote students' personal independence in routines and activities (e.g., picture schedules, transition objects, checklists, print or digital personal organizers, assignment notebooks, binders, calendars, daily planners).	Most team members use three or more strategies across classroom activities to promote students' personal independence (e.g., picture schedules, transition objects, checklists, print or digital personal organizers, assignment notebooks, binders, calendars, daily planners).

Figure 5.7. Item 24 from APERS-PE/SA addressing use of strategies to promote student independence.

Interfering Behavior

Some students with autism may engage in behavior that interferes with learning and participation in the school session. For those students, it may be necessary to develop a plan that addresses such behavior. Quality features of school programs that address interfering behavior include assessing the behavior to determine its function and designing a specific program that prevents, reduces, and/or replaces the behavior (i.e., with more functional behavior). If no interfering behaviors occur for students in the class, then the items that address functional assessment and developing a behavior program are not scored; although Item 26 addressing use of proactive strategies may still be scored. Figure 5.8 shows Item 27, which focuses on conducting an FBA as a step in designing a behavior program for students.

Item #27		
This is a challenge in our program.	This element is consistently in place, but we still have some work to do.	This is a real strength in our program.
When interfering behaviors occur, team members do not use a functional behavioral assessment (FBA) to understand the cause of the behavior.	When interfering behaviors occur, one member of the team conducts an FBA to determine the cause of the behavior. Team members observe the student and the interfering behavior in the context where the student displays the behavior (e.g., home, school, community) and include these observations in the FBA.	When interfering behaviors occur, team members conduct an FBA in collaboration with family members, generate a hypothesis statement in the FBA about the potential function(s) of the behavior (e.g., behavior serves as an escape or tangible/access function), and identify possible replacement behaviors that can serve as the focus of the intervention to reduce interfering behaviors.

Figure 5.8. Item 27 from APERS-PE/SA addressing use of functional behavioral assessments to manage interfering behavior.

Family Involvement

Involving families in school programs for their children and youth with autism is an essential feature of quality. Having an open and consistent mode of communication with family members, sharing information about their children and available resources, and including them in important decisions are key features. In Figure 5.9, Item 29 reflects the subdomain of Communication With Family in the APERS-PE/SA.

Item #29		
This is a challenge in our program.	This element is consistently in place, but we still have some work to do.	This is a real strength in our program.
Team members have limited communication with family outside of the IEP conference, and none speak plainly or provide explanation of technical terms to families during the IEP conference.	One team member communicates with parents by sending home weekly to monthly reports of activities in the classroom and avoids jargon and acronyms during communication.	One team member has a system for regular communication that is individualized to each family and is consistently used. Most team members avoid jargon and acronyms when communicating with parents/families, and when technical terms must be used, they are explained.

Figure 5.9.   Item 29 from APERS-PE/SA addressing communication with families.

Teaming

In high-quality programs, members from different disciplines contribute to the planning and delivery of instruction and intervention for students with autism. Such involvement requires that professionals work as a team, and this domain reflects such teamwork. The Teaming domain of the APERS-PE/SA focuses on team decision making and collaboration. In Figure 5.10, Item 32 reflects one feature of the teaming process.

Item #32		
This is a challenge in our program.	This element is consistently in place, but we still have some work to do.	This is a real strength in our program.
Team members (e.g., special education teacher) have no collaborative relationship with other team members (e.g., SLP). Team meetings are rare.	One team member has an ongoing collaborative relationship with at least two other team members and provides limited feedback, communication, and sharing of data (e.g., assessment data, ongoing data collected). Team meetings occur on an "as needed" basis, but more than two times a year.	One team member (e.g., special education teacher, SLP) is assigned and has an ongoing collaborative relationship with all team members. One team member provides effective feedback, frequent communication, and data with other team members (e.g., assessment data, ongoing data collected). Team meetings are scheduled at regular, predictable times throughout the school year.

Figure 5.10.   Item 32 from APERS-PE/SA addressing collaboration among team members.

PROCEDURES FOR COMPLETING THE APERS-PE SELF-ASSESSMENT TOOL

As previously stated, the APERS-PE/SA is designed for teachers to self-identify the strengths and challenges of their program for students with autism. Items are organized by domains that represent elements of program quality. Teachers should follow these instructions when using the APERS-PE/SA tools:

* *Review the instrument prior to completing.* This allows the opportunity to clarify the meaning of an item prior to rating it.

- *Set aside approximately 40–50 minutes to complete the self-assessment.* It is preferable that the ratings be completed in one sitting. If not feasible (e.g., because of class schedules, teaching responsibilities), then completing it over two sittings is acceptable as long as the full self-assessment is completed within 1 week. Because attention to the items is important, it is important to find a quiet space with few, if any, interruptions when completing the ratings.

- *Identify focus student(s) as reference for answering the self-assessment items.* Think about the student or students with autism in your classroom, and answer the items based on programming for this/these students. If you have an entire classroom of students with autism, then it might be useful to identify two or three students with varying needs who represent the characteristics of students in the class on which to base your responses.

- *For each self-assessment item, check the one box that corresponds with the statement that best describes your classroom or program for children or youth with autism.* You may add notes to better reflect the specifics about your program related to the item. This is optional but can be useful if you feel the item does not reflect an accurate picture of your program. Figure 5.11 provides an example of an item from the Learning Environments domain. In this item, the teacher is asked to rate how easily students' activities can be monitored in the classroom.

- *Review the self-assessment quality ratings for each domain.* The APERS-PE/SA will automatically generate a summary of the completed items and a graph of the array of ratings. This information is found on the "Summary" tab in the Self-Assessment Tool.

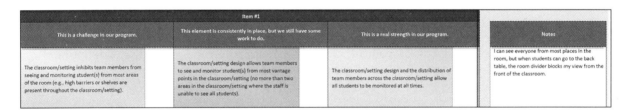

Figure 5.11. Sample Item 1 from APERS-PE/SA with notes.

IMPORTANT NOTE ABOUT THE SCORING TOOL: In order for the Scoring Tool to function correctly, macros must be enabled within the Excel file. Information on how to enable macros for this file can be found on the About the Downloads page.

USING THE APERS-PE SELF-ASSESSMENT PROGRAM RATINGS

The APERS-PE/SA Tool accompanying this manual will automatically generate quality rating for each domain. These ratings are displayed in the three categories previously mentioned. When each item is completed with a score, the rater will click on the "Summary" tab to view a summary rating profile for each domain (see Figure 5.12). Scores closer to "1" will represent challenges for the program, scores around "3" represent areas that need work, and scores high in the "4" to "5" range represent strengths of the program. If the rater has inadvertently not checked an item, "Incomplete" will show as the domain score, which will allow the rater to examine the domain and enter a code for the uncoded item(s). The program will provide a graphic profile of

Domain	Score
1. Learning Environments	4.2
2. Positive Learning Climate	3.7
3. Assessment and IEP Development	3.7
4. Curriculum and Instruction	4.0
5. Communication	3.0
6. Social Competence	2.3
7. Personal Independence and Competence	3.0
8. Interfering Behavior	3.0
9. Family Involvement	5.0
10. Teaming	4.0
Overall	3.6

Figure 5.12.   Example of summary results from the APERS-PE/SA.

the ratings (see Figure 5.13). This profile allows the rater to quickly see the quality features of the program that are strengths, those that are in place but need more work, and those that are challenges. We recommend the raters review the graphic profile for strengths, areas that need work, and challenges instead of the numerical values. The graphic displayed in Figure 5.13 is for a strong program. Many of the domains are above the mid-range (i.e., in place but needs work). Social Competence is the domain that fell below the mid-range and could be the area that is first identified for program improvement. Other instructional areas focusing on Communication, Personal Independence and Competence, and Interfering Behavior might also be targeted for program improvement.

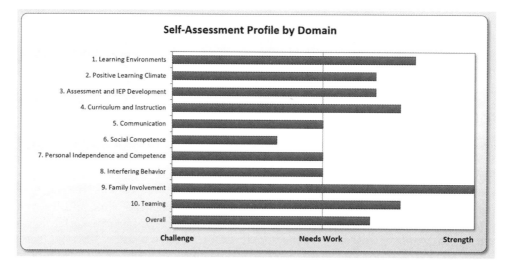

Figure 5.13.   Example of a graphic display from the APERS-PE/SA.

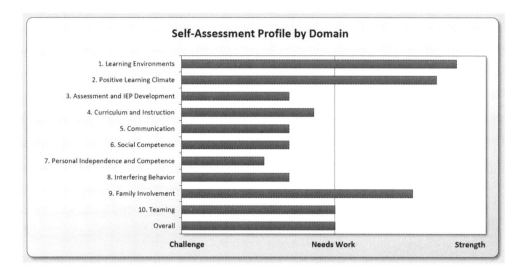

Figure 5.14. A second example of a graphic display from the APERS-PE/SA.

As noted in the previous chapter, the self-assessment is specifically designed to provide information that teachers or other service providers could use directly for self-improvement, rather than to provide a numeric score. Based on the teacher's reflections about their own practice, they could develop a plan for program quality improvement. Figure 5.14 shows another sample graph of APERS-PE/SA results for a program that is weaker than the one described in the previous paragraph. For the classroom depicted, the teacher rating identified Learning Environments, Positive Learning Climate, and Family Involvement as the strengths of the program. Yet, several domain scores fall below the mid-range: Assessment and IEP Development, Curriculum and Instruction, Communication, Social Competence, Personal Independence and Competence, and Interfering Behavior.

The three domains that appeared to need the most improvement are Assessment and IEP Development, Communication, and Personal Independence and Competence. For each of these domains, the teacher can look at the specific items on which they scored themselves the lowest. They could develop a plan for how to bring the practices identified in those domains up to at least the acceptable level (i.e., in place but still needs work). Such a plan might include changes that could be directly made in the classroom, changes that might occur with other team members, or the identification of resources needed to make the change. The latter is particularly important in that it could provide a basis for discussion with leadership in the school (e.g., principal, program director) or school system (e.g., district autism services coordinator) about resources needed to improve quality. The teacher could then follow a similar process to improve in other areas that are relatively weak—Curriculum and Instruction, Social Competence, and Interfering Behavior.

Using the APERS-PE Self-Assessment for Performance Review

Two other audiences exist for this self-assessment data. Teachers and their service providers are evaluated each year, often by the principal or other administrative personnel. Early in the year, teachers/service providers could share the APERS-PE/SA with their most direct supervisor and communicate a plan for program improvement based on their own self-assessment. Near the end of the year, teachers/service providers could complete the self-assessment a second time and share the information with their supervisor during or in preparation for their end-of-the-year evaluation. Providing such data on program improvement is a powerful statement about a teacher's performance.

Using the APERS-PE Self-Assessment for Communication With Families

Parents could be a second audience for information provided by the self-assessment. Although parents can see the structural features of the classroom when they come to visit, they may not know about the quality features of the program their autistic child or adolescent is receiving. Using the domains of the APERS-PE/SA to communicate to parents the features of the programs that are important and represent the educational services their child is receiving could be a valuable avenue for building the relationship between parents and school personnel.

SUMMARY

In this chapter, we have described the rating system for the APERS-PE/SA. The self-assessment domains parallel the full APERS-PE assessment but are briefer and intended to be used by teachers and other service providers in the program. The information generated by the self-assessments is designed to guide teachers and other service providers in program improvement plans. It can also be used as part of performance reviews for teachers and other service providers and as a tool for communicating with families about program features.

6 Understanding the Empirical Foundations and Research Uses of APERS

"Be a yardstick of quality. Some people aren't used to an environment where excellence is expected."

—Steve Jobs

Children and youth with autism spend a significant amount of time in public school program environments, day in and day out, for years of their lives. In Chapter 1, we described the importance of ensuring that such environments are of high quality, not only for the quality of life they may provide, but also for the foundation they establish on which effective instruction and intervention can be delivered. As such, assessment of educational environments is critical, but the assessments themselves must be of high quality, as measured through psychometric evaluations. In this chapter, we describe the psychometric qualities of the APERS (i.e., reliability and validity) documented by empirical research. We then take the next step of reporting how the APERS has been used in research to improve educational program environments and also suggest directions for future research.

As explained in Chapter 1, the APERS exists in two versions, one for preschool/elementary programs (APERS-PE) and one for middle/high school programs (APERS-MH). Psychometric analyses of the APERS have used both versions, which is described in the following sections.

PSYCHOMETRIC FEATURES OF THE APERS

Reliability and validity are the two fundamental psychometric features of any assessment instrument. Internal consistency (Henson, 2001), or how consistently items measure autism program quality, is the type of reliability analyzed for the APERS. Interrater agreement is a concept related to, but not exactly the same as, reliability, but also reflects a feature of the psychometric qualities of the scale (Suen & Ary, 1989). Validity is the degree to which the scale measures the construct that it proposes to measure (Nunnally & Bernstein, 1994). APERS investigators have examined two forms of validity—construct validity (i.e., how well the scale items cohere in capturing the main construct) and criterion-related validity (i.e., the degree to which the scale discriminates between groups as intended in a proposed hypothesis). The research presented in this section was previously published in Odom et al. (2018).

Program Samples

The psychometric analyses were drawn from the NPDC evaluation study, discussed in Chapter 1, and from an efficacy study of the comprehensive treatment model for the CSESA. (Note that in the earlier APERS versions used in these studies, domain names and order differ slightly from the current APERS-PE and APERS-MH; for details, see table and figure descriptions throughout this chapter.)

NPDC Sample   As noted earlier, the NPDC worked with states to design a system of professional development to improve programs for children and youth with autism, and the NPDC investigators used the APERS-PE and APERS-MH to evaluate outcomes. Data from the NPDC sample were collected in 72 school-based programs located in 11 states (California, Idaho, Indiana, Kentucky, Michigan, Minnesota, New Mexico, Rhode Island, Texas, Virginia, Vermont, Wisconsin). The sample included inclusive and self-contained special education classes for children and youth with autism at the preschool, elementary, middle school, and high school levels. NPDC program staff collected the APERS data at the beginning of the school year and again at the end of the school year. More information about this sample can be found in Odom et al. (2013).

CSESA Sample   CSESA conducted a randomized clinical trial of a school-based comprehensive treatment model in a larger study that is described in a subsequent section. The CSESA sample was drawn from 60 high school programs located in California, North Carolina, and Wisconsin (none of these were in the NPDC sample, and all data were from the pretest APERS-MH). The programs were inclusive ($n = 56$) and self-contained special education ($n = 43$) (i.e., the total number exceeds 60 because some inclusive and special education programs were in the same high school). In this study, CSESA staff, who were not coaches in the high school assessed, administered the APERS-MH at the beginning of a school year and then again at the end of the next school year (i.e., approximately 18 months after the first administration).

Interrater Agreement

The NPDC project was a professional development project, and program staff were not able to collect interrater agreement data because of limited funds. Interrater agreement data was collected, however, for the CSESA project (see Kraemer et al., 2020). Two CSESA staff simultaneously observed, conducted interviews, reviewed documents, and then independently scored the APERS-MH in 21 high schools (35% of the sample). The items-level ratings were then compared, generating agreement percentages for each observation. The average exact agreement (i.e., number of items each rater scored the same rating divided by the total number of items) was 76.5%, and agreement within 1 point was 95.2%, respectively. In addition, the average item ratings for the total APERS scores for the two raters was 3.31 and 3.33, respectively. Also, data on the difference between the two raters on individual items were collected (e.g., if the first rater scored a 3 on Item 1 and the second rater scored a 4, then the difference was 1). The average difference between the two raters on individual items was .37 (i.e., out of a rating system that went from 1.00 to 5.00). Last, the interclass correlation and Pearson Product Moment correlation between the two raters were .56 and .54, respectively.

Reliability

Reliability of an assessment instrument refers to how consistently an assessment instrument is measuring the thing for which it was designed, which for the APERS is program quality. Iternal consistency is one type of reliability. For both the NPDC and CSESA samples, investigators from the respective projects calculated Cronbach alphas to assess internal consistency. For the NPDC sample, separate alphas occurred for both forms of the APERS (PE and MH) and also for inclusive and self-contained classes. For the CSESA sample, calculations only occurred for the inclusive and special education programs. These data are presented in

Table 6.1. Internal consistency of the APERS for NPDC and CSESA

	NPDC				CSESA	
	P/E	MHS	Incl	S/C	Incl	S/C
Total	.96	.96	.96	.94	.95	.96
Learning Environments	.69	.71	.76	.73	.82	.81
Positive Learning Climate	.76	.78	.61	.77	.71	.68
Assessment and IEP Development	.84	.87	.86	.86	.60	.76
Curriculum and Instruction	.81	.77	.85	.84	.87	.89
Communication	.79	.92	.84	.73	.69	.74
Social	.72	.78	.73	.63	.70	.75
Personal Independence and Competence	.75	.78	.75	.76	.70	.75
Functional Behavior	.85	.81	.76	.68	.81	.81
Family Involvement	.88	.76	.78	.68	.74	.68
Teaming	.85	.71	.72	.74	.68	.60

From Odom, S. L., Cox, A., Sideris, J., Hume, K. A., Hedges, S., Kucharczyk, S., Shaw, E., Boyd, B. A., Reszka, S., & Neitzel, J. (2018). Assessing quality of program environments for children and youth with autism: Autism Program Environment Rating Scale. *Journal of Autism and Developmental Disorders, 48*, 913-924; reprinted by permission.

Two domains listed have been renamed in the current versions of the APERS-PE and APERS-MH: Social–Social Competence, Functional Behavior–Interfering Behavior.

Key: P/E, APERS-PE; MHS, APERS-MH; Incl, inclusive settings; S/C, self-contained.

Table 6.1. Alpha coefficients for total score were quite high, ranging from .94 to .96. The scores for the domains were lower, generally in the .70–.80 range. It should be noted that such lower scores are expected because the analysis is sensitive to the number of items in the analysis (i.e., the smaller the number of items, the lower the coefficients tend to be), and the domains had a smaller number of items than the total score analysis.

Validity

Validity refers to how well an assessment instrument is measuring the thing for which it was designed. Construct validity is one type of validity, which examines if items on an assessment are measuring a single thing or multiple things. To assess construct validity, the statistician on the APERS team conducted a confirmatory factor analysis (CFA) with the NPDC data and then replicated the analysis with the CSESA data. A one factor solution (i.e., program quality) was tested (i.e., the hypothesized relationship) in each analysis. The CFA confirmed a model fit for a single factor for the NPDC data, which was replicated in a second analysis of the CSESA data. Factor loadings of the domains on the single factor appear in Tables 6.2 and 6.3.

Criterion-related validity is a second type of validity in which an assessment generates outcomes that is consistent with a hypothesis or prediction. Teachers in the NPDC study participated in professional development and coaching with the hypothesis that APERS scores would increase from pretest to posttest. (This hypothesis is described more fully in a subsequent section.) To detect changes across the school year, the statistician on the APERS team conducted univariate t tests for the total score and the domain scores (see Table 6.4). These pre-post differences were significant at the $p < .001$. The total score effect size was 1.08, with the domain effect sizes ranging from 0.50 to 1.09. These findings indicate that the APERS is sensitive to change over time, which is consistent with the stated hypothesis of the study.

Cultural content validity is another type of validity in which items are judged to be measuring the same thing when an assessment is used in another country or culture. The APERS is a very U.S.-centric instrument. It was developed in the United States, and some of the items were designed to conform with the special education laws in the United States. Bejnö et al. (2019) conducted a cross-cultural content validation to adapt the APERS for use in preschools in Sweden and possibly other Nordic countries. They first translated the APERS-PE into Swedish.

Table 6.2. Factor loadings for the NPDC sample

APERS domains	One factor
Learning Environment Structure/Schedule	0.61
Positive Learning Climate	0.63
Assessment and IEP Development	0.72
Curriculum and Instruction	0.87
Communication	0.67
Social	0.68
Personal Independence and Competence	0.79
Functional Behavior (interfering and adaptive)	0.67
Family Involvement	0.57
Teaming	0.61
Model fit	
Degrees of freedom	35
Chi square	149.81 $p = .0000$
RMSEA	0.14
CFI	0.87

From Odom, S. L., Cox, A., Sideris, J., Hume, K. A., Hedges, S., Kucharczyk, S., Shaw, E., Boyd, B. A., Reszka, S., & Neitzel, J. (2018). Assessing quality of program environments for children and youth with autism: Autism Program Environment Rating Scale. *Journal of Autism and Developmental Disorders, 48*, 913-924; reprinted by permission.

Three domains listed have been renamed in the current versions of the APERS-PE and APERS-MH: Learning Environment Structure/Schedule–Learning Environments, Social–Social Competence, Functional Behavior–Interfering Behavior.

Table 6.3. Factor loadings for the CSESA sample

APERS domains	With clustering	Ignoring clustering
Learning Environment Structure/Schedule	0.71	0.62
Positive Learning Climate	0.60	0.63
Assessment and IEP Development	0.49	0.61
Curriculum and Instruction	0.83	0.89
Communication	0.68	0.77
Social	0.26	0.61
Personal Independence and Competence	0.69	0.75
Functional Behavior (interfering and adaptive)	0.72	0.63
Family Involvement	0.40	0.50
Teaming	0.43	0.59
Model fit		
Degrees of freedom	70	35
Chi square	152.74 $p = .0000$	70.21 $p = .0004$
RMSEA	0.11	0.10
CFI	0.83	0.92

From Odom, S. L., Cox, A., Sideris, J., Hume, K. A., Hedges, S., Kucharczyk, S., Shaw, E., Boyd, B. A., Reszka, S., & Neitzel, J. (2018). Assessing quality of program environments for children and youth with autism: Autism Program Environment Rating Scale. *Journal of Autism and Developmental Disorders, 48*, 913-924; reprinted by permission.

Three domains listed have been renamed in the current versions of the APERS-PE and APERS-MH: Learning Environment Structure/Schedule–Learning Environments, Social–Social Competence, Functional Behavior–Interfering Behavior.

They then modified the scale to focus only on the preschool content, had five preschool and early intervention experts provide feedback, and adapted the scale based on their feedback (i.e., dropped individual items in several domains, modified terminology). The resulting adapted scale was called the APERS-P-SE. Following a standard content validity process, Bejnö et al. had nine different experts, who were not in the first group of reviewers, complete the Content

Table 6.4. Changes across time for programs in NPDC study

| | Point estimates | | | | | | | |
| | Pre | | | Post | | | | |
APERS domains	N	Mean	Std	N	Mean	Std	t	d
Total	68	3.50	0.61	66	4.16	0.46	9.77***	1.08
Learning Environment Structure/Schedule	68	3.99	0.63	66	4.47	0.44	6.84***	0.76
Positive Learning Climate	68	3.93	0.84	66	4.40	0.58	4.38***	0.56
Assessment and IEP Development	68	3.43	0.83	66	4.13	0.58	7.70***	0.84
Curriculum and Instruction	68	3.35	0.71	66	4.09	0.64	9.52***	1.04
Communication	68	2.47	0.96	66	3.50	0.98	6.80***	1.07
Social	68	3.00	0.81	66	3.88	0.87	8.16***	1.09
Staff/Peer Relationships	68	2.95	0.96	66	3.76	0.82	6.57***	0.84
Personal Independence and Competence	67	3.58	0.91	66	4.17	0.80	5.48***	0.65
Functional Behavior	68	4.20	0.80	66	4.60	0.56	6.04***	0.50
Family Involvement	68	3.80	0.69	66	4.38	0.51	7.08***	0.84

Source: Odom et al. (2013).

***$p < .001$

Several domains listed have been renamed in the current versions of the APERS-PE and APERS-MH: Learning Environment Structure/Schedule–Learning Environments, Social and Staff/Peer Relationships–both part of Social Competence, Functional Behavior–Interfering Behavior.

Validity Index. These experts rated each item for clarity, comprehensiveness, and relevance. The overall ratings were 2.78 (out of 3.0) for item clarity, 2.82 for comprehensiveness, and 2.88 for relevance. These ratings documented the content validity of the APERS for the Swedish preschool context. The formative feedback from the last group of experts indicated the importance of the scale for preschool programs in Sweden that enroll children with autism, the distance between current practice and high ratings of quality on the APERS, and the challenge of collecting the APERS data in preschool settings because of the labor intensiveness.

NPDC AND THE FIRST USE OF APERS IN RESEARCH AND EVALUATION

The goal of the NPDC was to promote the use of evidence-based practices in school-based programs for students with autism, from preschool to high school. As previously noted, an assumption of the NPDC model was that implementation of evidence-based practices was difficult or impossible unless a certain level of quality exists in classroom programs. For example, trying to employ discrete trial training or naturalistic intervention is nearly impossible in classrooms where there is not a predictable routine, a stable classroom organization, and some level of visual support. Gathering APERS assessment information and working with teachers to improve quality was essential in the NPDC model. As such, an important evaluation question was, "Does the use of the NPDC model result in a positive change in the quality of the classroom or school program environment?"

The NPDC evaluation study was reported in Odom et al. (2013) and briefly described in the previous section on validity, so the procedures and findings will only be summarized here. Staff from the NPDC worked with staff from 12 states to support their use of the NPDC model. Leadership in each state had recruited three model classrooms for the first year and three for the second year to participate in the NPDC model. In each state, NPDC staff trained state-level coaches to conduct the APERS. NPDC staff held a training academy for teachers and state coaches during the summer of the year the NPDC model was implemented. The NPDC model, including the APERS, was introduced in the academy. Other aspects of the training focused on student goal identification and selection of evidence-based practices to address the goal. At the beginning of the school year, NPDC staff and state-level coaches conducted the APERS, wrote a report of the results, shared the information with the school staff, and developed an action plan to improve the program quality. NPDC staff and the state-level coaches then worked with the

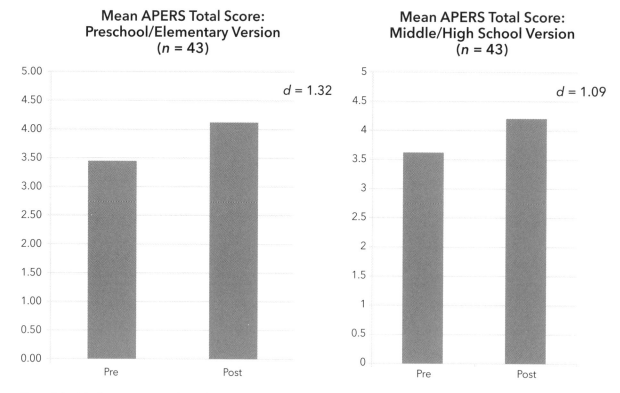

Figure 6.1.   NPDC mean item rating for total APERS (PE and MH). (*Source:* Odom et al., 2013.)

teachers to support the implementation of the action plan. At the same time, NPDC staff and coaches supported the teachers use of evidence-based practices directed to individualized child goals. At the end of the year, NPDC staff and state-level coaches again conducted the APERS to document changes across the year.

It is important to note that the data presented in this chapter differ slightly from those reported in Odom et al. (2013). The article contained data from classrooms in nine states, which were the data available at the time. NPDC worked in a total of 12 states, and we present APERS data from classrooms in all states in this chapter. The APERS scores are displayed as average item ratings (i.e., with a range of 1 to 5). The total APERS score across all items was 3.53 at pretest and 4.17 at posttest. We found several things when we examined the scores on the domains. These data are presented in Figures 6.1 and 6.2. First, scores on some domains are higher than others at pretest. The Class Environment, Family Involvement, and Teaming domains tended to be higher than the other, instruction-oriented domains such as Assessment, Curriculum and Instruction, Social Competence, Communication, Personal Independence, and Functional Behavior. This is a characteristic pattern that we find in many classes and schools (Hume et al., 2022; Odom et al., 2022). Second, as indicated in the previous validity section, the APERS ratings at posttest were significantly higher than pretest.

EVALUATING THE NPDC MODEL WHEN IMPLEMENTED IN ELEMENTARY SCHOOLS

The program evaluation of NPDC suggested that improvement in program quality occurred when the teachers used the program for 1 year. We could not include a control group in that evaluation study, however, because of financial constraints (i.e., it was a professional development center and had limited funds for program evaluation). Rhe Institute of Education Sciences

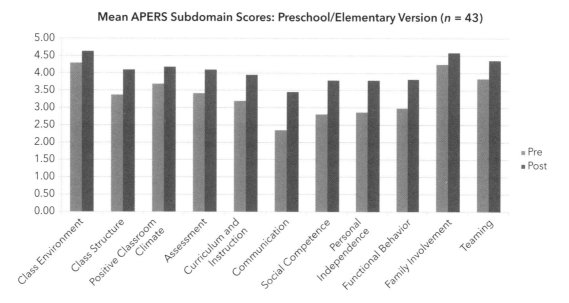

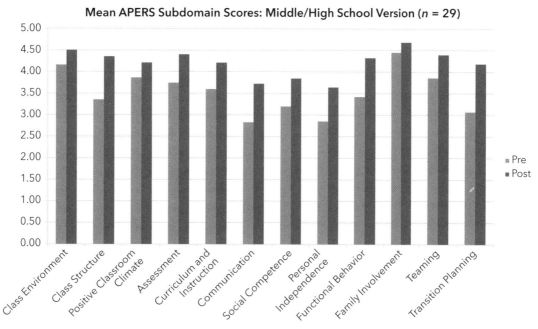

Figure 6.2. NPDC mean item ratings for domains of APERS-PE and APERS-MH. *Note:* Several domains listed have been renamed in the current versions of the APERS-PE and APERS-MH: Class Environment, Class Structure–both part of Learning Environments; Positive Classroom Climate–Positive Learning Climate; Assessment–Assessment and IEP Development; Functional Behavior–Interfering Behavior. (From Odom, S. L., Cox, A., & Brock, M. [2013]. Implementation science, professional development, and autism spectrum disorders: National Professional Development Center on ASD. *Exceptional Children, 79,* 233–251; reprinted by permission.)

funded The Efficacy Study of Elementary Learners with Autism Spectrum Disorder (TESELA) to determine the efficacy of the NPDC model in elementary schools. This study took place in 60 elementary schools in a southeastern state. This study allowed us to address two questions:

1. What is the quality of elementary school programs for children with autism in this state?

2. Does the NPDC model improve the quality of elementary school programs in comparison with a Services as Usual (SAU) model?

Quality of Elementary School Programs

At the beginning of the school year, research staff, who were not serving as coaches in the schools being assessed, conducted the APERS-PE for all 60 schools in the study. Most of the schools had both inclusive and special education programs. The 60 schools were distributed across city, suburban, and rural areas in a southeastern state in the United States. An analysis of the demographics of the school using the Generalizer program (Tipton, 2014) revealed that this sample of schools were highly representative of the demographics of schools in the United States. This pretest data could, therefore, provide a glimpse into the quality programs for students with autism in the United States.

For this study, we assessed the reliability of the APERS-PE by calculating Cronbach alphas on total and domain scores (reported in Odom et al., 2022). Also, a second rater simultaneously conducted the APERS-PE for 20% of the schools, and we calculated interrater agreement using intraclass correlations (see Table 6.5). The internal consistency coefficients for the total scores for both inclusive and special education programs were above .90, with individual domain scores ranging from .55 to .89. Similarly, intraclass coefficients for the total APERS-PE were above .96 for both types of programs, with coefficients ranging from .57 to .97.

Table 6.5. Internal consistency and interclass correlations for APERS-PE for inclusive (IN) and special education (SE) elementary school settings

| Domain | Standardized Cronbach alpha | | ICCs | |
| | Program type | | Program type | |
	IN	SE	IN	SE
Assessment and IEP Development	0.551936	0.589340	0.90760	0.94711
Positive Learning Climate	0.818910	0.681591	0.53854	0.94164
Communication	0.598310	0.771864	0.70951	0.80076
Learning Environments	0.780271	0.847222	0.92811	0.97509
Family Involvement	0.693815	0.789309	0.91427	0.93064
Functional Behavior	0.765214	0.811414	0.86427	0.85450
Personal Independence and Competence	0.667507	0.737835	0.97907	0.88814
Curriculum and Instruction	0.879605	0.885416	0.86927	0.94815
Social Competence	0.668130	0.708708	0.93147	0.93132
Teaming	0.647042	0.717966	0.85227	0.85365
Overall	0.930945	0.960501	0.96549	0.97973

From Odom, S. L., Sam, A. M., Tomaszewski, B., & Cox, A. W. (2022). Quality of educational programs for elementary school-age students with autism. *American Journal on Intellectual and Developmental Disabilities, 127*(1), 29–41. Reprinted with permission.

The Functional Behavior domain is renamed Interfering Behavior in current versions of the APERS.

The APERS-PE scores for the 60 schools in the sample appear in Figure 6.3. The rating score of 3.0 was established as the benchmark for acceptable quality, and the overall quality of programs was close to this benchmark. We then compared specific domain scores to the benchmark. As can be seen, quality of the school environment, climate, and family communication were significantly above the benchmark. These domain reflect the concept of structural quality identified in in the previous research on early childhood education programs (National Institute of Child Health and Human Development, 2006). Other domains that represent more the process or instructional quality of the programs (i.e., Communication, Social, Independence, Functional Behavior) were significantly below the quality benchmark. In addition, we found a significant negative association between school percentage of children qualifying for free or reduced lunch (i.e., a proxity for low income). Last, we examined the differences between inclusive and special education programs (see Figure 6.4). Hierarchical linear modeling was used

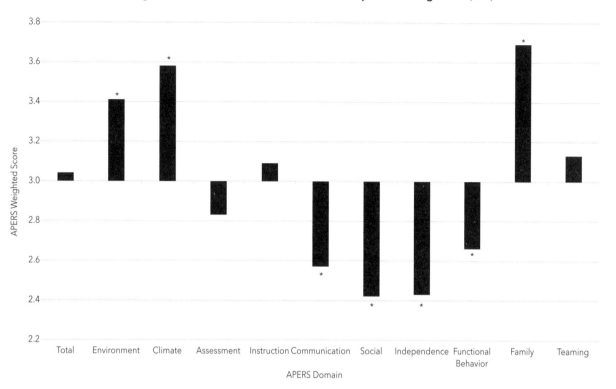

Mean Item Rating for Total Score and Domains With Acceptable Rating Score (3.0) as Referent

Note: APERS = Autism Program Environment Quality Rating Systems–Preschool/Elementary.
*Indicates significantly different from 3.0 (minimally acceptable) rating.

Figure 6.3. APERS-PE means ratings for all classes. *Note:* Several domains listed have been renamed in the current versions of the APERS-PE and APERS-MH: Environment–Learning Environments, Climate–Positive Learning Climate, Assessment–Assessment and IEP Development, Instruction–Curriculum and Instruction, Social–Social Competence, Independence–Personal Independence and Competence, Functional Behavior–Interfering Behavior, Family–Family Involvement. (From Odom, S. L., Sam, A. M., Tomaszewski, B., & Cox, A. W. [2022]. Quality of educational programs for elementary school-age students with autism. *American Journal on Intellectual and Developmental Disabilities, 127*[1], 29–41. Reprinted with permission.)

to control for nesting within schools, revealing that mean ratings did not differ for inclusive and special education programs for most domains. The two exceptions were that inclusive programs had significantly higher mean ratings compared with special education programs for the Social Domain, and special education programs had higher mean ratings than inclusive programs for the Assessment Domain.

Effects of NPDC

To determine the effects of the NPDC program, we randomly assigned the schools just described to an NPDC condition or an SAU condition (Sam et al., 2021). The assignment was on a 2:1 ratio, with 40 schools assigned to the NPDC and 20 to the SAU conditions. The NPDC model was designed to improve program quality in elementary schools in order for this program quality to serve as a platform for teachers' implementation of evidence-based practices. In the NPDC model, teachers attended an academy in the summer to learn about autism, the APERS, evidence-based practices, and writing observable and measurement goals. The school staff formed an Autism Team that consisted generally of teachers and staff who attended the summer academy and other school staff who would be implementing the NPDC program. After research staff completed the APERS-PE, they shared the information with the Autism Team. This team then established an action plan for promoting quality in their school as well as selecting and implementing evidence-based practices with individual students. Each school had an

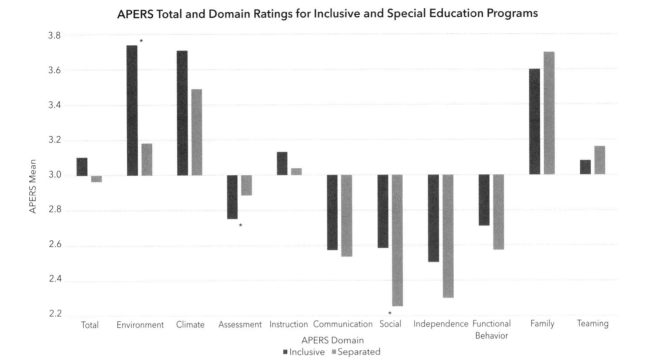

Note. APERS = Autism Program Environment Quality Rating Systems-Preschool/Elementary; IN = inclusive; SE = special education.
*Indicates significant difference between group.

Figure 6.4. APERS-PE means ratings for inclusive and special education classes in a southeastern state. *Note:* Several domains listed have been renamed in the current versions of the APERS-PE and APERS-MH: Environment–Learning Environments, Climate–Positive Learning Climate, Assessment–Assessment and IEP Development, Instruction–Curriculum and Instruction, Social–Social Competence, Independence–Personal Independence and Competence, Functional Behavior–Interfering Behavior, Family–Family Involvement. (From Odom, S. L., Sam, A. M., Tomaszewski, B., & Cox, A. W. [2022]. Quality of educational programs for elementary school-age students with autism. *American Journal on Intellectual and Developmental Disabilities, 127*[1], 29–41. Reprinted with permission.)

NPDC coach who spent 1 day a week at the school, with the focus on supporting school staff's efforts to improve program quality and deliver evidence-based practices.

The school in the SAU condition also formed an Autism Team. They were provided with information about autism, received the APERS information about program quality in their school, developed measurable and observable goals for their students, and received information about evidence-based practices. They did not receive further coaching or support from NPDC staff, however, after this initial introduction. In both sets of schools, the research staff also completed the APERS-PE at the end of the year.

The hypothesis related to Question 2 was that there would be significantly more positive changes in program quality across the academic year for schools in the NPDC group compared with schools in the SAU group. Actually, we found that program quality improved for both NPDC and SAU schools across the year, with no significant differences between groups (Sam et al., 2021). When we used an analysis of covariance to adjust the posttest ratings based on the pretest ratings, we found a pattern in which the NPDC schools consistently had higher ratings (at posttest) than the SAU schools, with substantial between-group standardized effect sizes favoring the NPDC group (see Figure 6.5). Given the magnitude of the Hedges' *g* effect sizes, we think that the lack of a significant finding may have been due to the relatively small number of schools in the sample.

The promising pattern of effect sizes led us to do a more fine-grained, separate analysis of the data from the inclusive and self-contained special education programs in the schools. We found significant differences in APERS-PE changes across the year (in this case revealed by time by treatment condition repeated measures ANOVA) favoring the NPDC schools for the

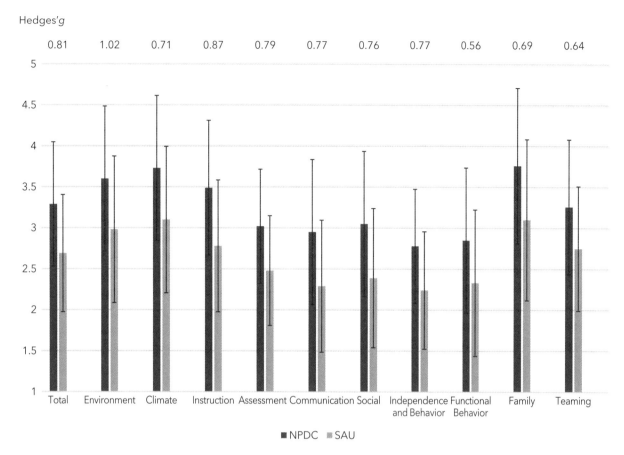

Figure 6.5. Adjusted posttest APERS means for TESELA and SAU schools with Hedges' *g* effect sizes and ranges of scores. *Note:* Several domains listed have been renamed in the current versions of the APERS-PE and APERS-MH: Environment–Learning Environments, Climate–Positive Learning Climate, Instruction–Curriculum and Instruction, Assessment–Assessment and IEP Development, Social–Social Competence, Independence and Behavior–Personal Independence and Competence, Functional Behavior–Interfering Behavior, Family–Family Involvement. (From Sam, A. M., Odom, S. L., Tomaszewski, B., Perkins, Y., & Cox, A. W. [2021]. Employing evidence-based practices for children with autism in elementary schools. *Journal of Autism and Developmental Disorders, 51*[7], 2308–2323. https://doi.org/10.1007/s10803-020-04706-x; reprinted by permission.)

inclusive programs but not for the self-contained special education programs. So, there appears to be a positive change in program quality in elementary schools as measured by the APER-PE resulting from the NPDC program (Sam et al., 2021).

EVALUATING CHANGES IN PROGRAM QUALITY IN THE EFFICACY STUDY OF THE CSESA

To support adolescents with autism enrolled in high schools, the Institute of Education Sciences funded the CSESA to develop a comprehensive program model. The CSESA project took place in 60 high schools located in three geographical areas in the United States (i.e., Southeast, Midwest, West Coast). An analysis of the geographic locations of the schools using the Generalizer program (Tipton, 2014) revealed that this sample of schools was highly representative of schools in the United States in terms of urbanicity, socioeconomic status, and race/ethnicity.

Quality of High School Programs in the United States

The APERS-MH was collected in all schools at the beginning of the study, which allowed us to obtain a glimpse of the existing quality of high school programs for autistic students that we felt was reflective of the quality in the United States (Kraemer et al., 2020). The overall APERS score was slightly above the 3.0 level, which we have proposed as adequate quality (see Figure 6.6).

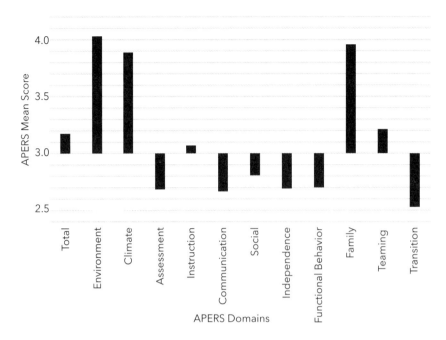

Figure 6.6. APERS-MH mean ratings for high school programs. *Note:* Several domains listed have been renamed in the current versions of the APERS-PE and APERS-MH: Environment–Learning Environments, Climate–Positive Learning Climate, Assessment–Assessment and IEP Development, Instruction–Curriculum and Instruction, Social–Social Competence, Independence–Personal Independence and Competence, Functional Behavior–Interfering Behavior, Family–Family Involvement. (From Kraemer, B. R., Odom, S. L., Tomaszewski, B., Hall, L. J., Dawalt, L., Hume, K. A., Steinbrenner, J. R., Szidon, K., & Brum, C. [2019]. Quality of high school programs for students with autism spectrum disorder. *Autism: The International Journal of Research and Practice, 24*[3], 707-717. https://doi .org/10.1177/1362361319887280; reprinted by permission.)

There were differences in domains, however. As noted for elementary school programs, the more structural features of program environment (e.g., Environment, School Climate, Family) appeared strong in high schools. The process features, which focused on instruction, intervention, and learning, were substantially lower than the 3.0 benchmark. Most important, preparation for transition scored the lowest of all domains.

Both inclusive (Standard Diploma) and self-contained special education (Modified Diploma) programs operated in most high schools. We compared the quality of each of these program types (Figure 6.7 and Table 6.6), and they were equivalent on nearly all domains, with four exceptions. The Assessment, Teaming, and Family domains were significantly higher for the special education program compared with the inclusive programs. Most important, quality in the special education programs was significantly higher than occurred for the special education programs for the Transition domain; although transition and assessment quality was still below the 3.0 level for both types of programs.

Improving Quality of High School Programs for Adolescents With Autism

The CSESA program (Hume et al., 2022), like the NPDC program, was built on the assumption that a foundational level of program quality was necessary for any program to be successfully implemented. In addition to building program quality, there were four intervention features, focusing on academics (i.e., primarily literacy), social competence, independence, and transition/families. The high schools just described were randomly assigned to CSESA and SAU conditions, and a total of 545 autistic students participated in the study. As with the TESELA study, the APERS was collected for the entire school rather than at the individual classroom level.

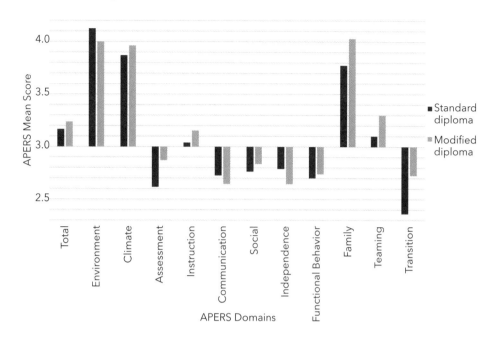

Figure 6.7. APERS-MH mean ratings for inclusive and special education programs. *Note:* Several domains listed have been renamed in the current versions of the APERS-PE and APERS-MH: Environment–Learning Environments, Climate–Positive Learning Climate, Assessment–Assessment and IEP Development, Instruction–Curriculum and Instruction, Social–Social Competence, Independence–Personal Independence and Competence, Functional Behavior–Interfering Behavior, Family–Family Involvement. (From Kraemer, B. R., Odom, S. L., Tomaszewski, B., Hall, L. J., Dawalt, L., Hume, K. A., Steinbrenner, J. R., Szidon, K., & Brum, C. [2019]. Quality of high school programs for students with autism spectrum disorder. *Autism: The International Journal of Research and Practice, 24*[3], 707-717. https://doi.org/10.1177/1362361319887280; reprinted by permission.)

Table 6.6. Differences in APERS scores for inclusive (standard diploma) and special education (modified diploma) in high school settings

APERS domain	Standard diploma program, mean (SD) (N = 60)	Modified diploma program, mean (SD) (N = 47)	β (group parameter estimate [SE])	t-value (DF = 46)	p-value	Effect size
Total	3.17 (0.46)	3.24 (0.54)	0.03 (0.07)	0.49	0.63	0.07
Environment	4.13 (0.62)	4.01 (0.67)	−0.16 (0.10)	1.56	0.13	0.25
Climate	3.87 (0.80)	3.96 (0.78)	0.09 (0.10)	0.60	0.55	0.12
Assessment	2.62 (0.53)	2.87 (0.65)	0.20 (0.09)	2.28	0.03	0.34
Instruction	3.04 (0.67)	3.15 (0.73)	0.07 (0.10)	0.73	0.47	0.10
Communication	2.72 (0.81)	2.65 (0.77)	−0.09 (0.12)	0.76	0.45	0.12
Social	2.77 (0.65)	2.84 (0.72)	0.10 (0.09)	1.07	0.29	0.14
Independence	2.79 (0.62)	2.65 (0.74)	−0.18 (0.11)	1.66	0.10	0.27
Functional Behavior	2.70 (0.81)	2.74 (0.72)	0.004 (0.11)	0.05	0.97	0.01
Family	3.77 (0.88)	4.03 (0.82)	0.27 (0.13)	2.05	0.05	0.33
Teaming	3.10 (0.54)	3.30 (0.53)	0.22 (0.08)	2.88	0.006	0.40
Transition	2.36 (0.53)	2.72 (0.68)	0.36 (0.08)	4.44	<0.001	0.58

From Kraemer, B. R., Odom, S. L., Tomaszewski, B., Hall, L. J., Dawalt, L., Hume, K. A., Steinbrenner, J. R., Szidon, K., & Brum, C. (2019). Quality of high school programs for students with autism spectrum disorder. *Autism: The International Journal of Research and Practice, 24*(3), 707-717; adapted by permission.

Several domains listed have been renamed in the current versions of the APERS-PE and APERS-MH: Environment–Learning Environments, Climate–Positive Learning Climate, Assessment–Assessment and IEP Development, Instruction–Curriculum and Instruction, Social–Social Competence, Independence–Personal Independence and Competence, Functional Behavior–Interfering Behavior, Family–Family Involvement.

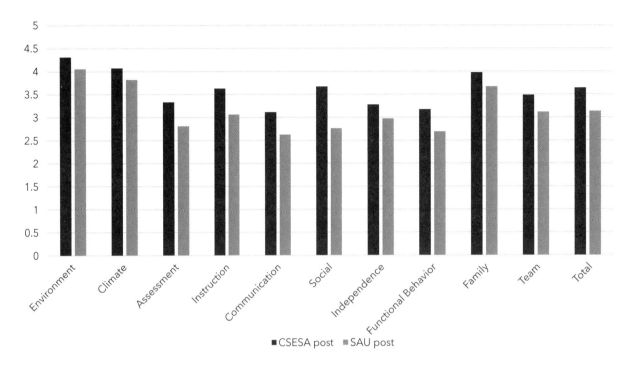

Figure 6.8. APERS-MH posttest mean scores adjusted based on pretest for CSESA and SAU schools. Significant difference between groups for Assessment (*p* = .003, *d* = .793), Instruction (*p* < .001, *d* = .974), Communication (*p* = .009, *d* = .688), Social (*p* < .001, *d* = 1.43), Independence (*p* < .010, *d* = .686), Functional Behavior (*p* = .016, *d* = .683), Team (*p* < .010, *d* = .701). *Note:* Several domains listed have been renamed in the current versions of the APERS-PE and APERS-MH: Environment–Learning Environments, Climate–Positive Learning Climate, Assessment–Assessment and IEP Development, Instruction–Curriculum and Instruction, Social–Social Competence, Independence–Personal Independence and Competence, Functional Behavior–Interfering Behavior, Family–Family Involvement, Team–Teaming. (From Hume, K., Odom, S. L., Steinbrenner, J. R., DaWalt, L. S., Hall, L. J., Kraemer, B., Tomaszewski, B., Brum, C., Szidon, K., & Bolt, D. [2022]. Efficacy of a school-based comprehensive intervention program for adolescents with autism. *Exceptional Children, 88*[2], 223–240. https://doi.org/10.1177/00144029211062589; adapted by permission.)

At the beginning of the school year, research staff shared the APERS-MH information for their school with an Autism Team formed at each school. Research staff in the CSESA schools also worked with the Autism Team to develop an action plan for improving program quality. During a 2-year period, CSESA coaches supported CSESA school staff through training on each of the intervention features previously noted, as well as coaching implementation about 1 day a week. The APERS was collected in all schools at the end of the 2-year period. In general, SAU schools did not have changes in quality across the 2-year period, whereas CSESA schools showed significant improvements in quality. The adjusted posttest means (covarying for pretest) appear in Figure 6.8. There were significant differences between groups for Assessment and IEP Development (*p* =.003, *d* =.793), Curriculum and Instruction (*p* < .001, *d* = .974), Communication (*p* = .009, *d* = .688), Social Competence (*p* < .001, *d* = 1.43), Personal Independence and Competence (*p* < .010, *d* = .686), Interfering Behavior (*p* = .016, *d* = .683), and Teaming (*p* = .010, *d* = .701). We created a composite score from all the items in the APERS-MH that related to transition (i.e., the current APERS-MH has a separate transition domain, but the version of the APERS-MH used for the CSESA study did not) to more directly assess quality differences in the transition area, which is of considerable importance for high school students. Overall, the CSESA scores made significant positive changes in the transition area, with mean scores exceeding 3.0, and were significantly different from the SAU schools (which remained below the 3.0 level) at posttest.

USING APERS TO PROMOTE PROGRAM QUALITY IN SWEDEN

In Sweden, Bejnö, Roll-Petterssen, et al. (2021) examined the use of the APERS in combination with the delivery of an early intensive behavioral intervention (EIBI) program. In a quasi-experimental design study, the APERS-PE-S was conducted at the beginning of the study and again 8 months later. In one group, children with autism enrolled in community preschool

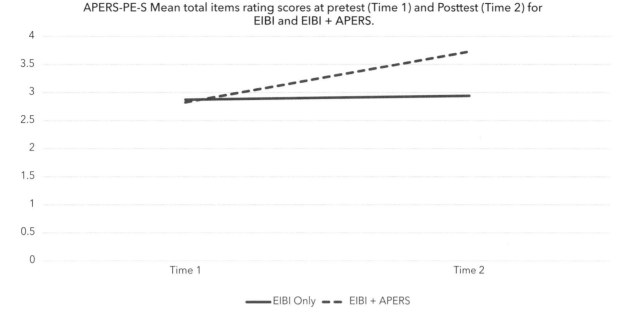

Figure 6.9. APERS-PE-S mean total items rating scores at pretest (Time 1) and posttest (Time 2) for EIBI and EIBI + APERS. (*Source:* Bejnö et al., 2021).

programs received the EIBI program delivered by a paraeducator in the preschool setting and supervised by a behavior therapist at a central clinic. The second group also received the EIBI program as well as information about program quality generated by the pretest APERS assessment and coaching to change the quality of the program. Employing a repeated measures analysis of variance, the change in the total APERS-PE-S mean rating was significantly greater (i.e., a time by treatment interaction) for the APERS group compared with the EIBI-only group ($p < .003$; partial $eta^2 = .47$; See Figure 6.9). In addition, there were significant differences on the Environment ($p = .002$, partial $eta^2 = .55$) and Personal Independence ($p < .004$, partial $eta^2 = .51$) domains. At the end of the research study, this research team interviewed leaders of the preschool programs who had received the EIBI + APERS conditions, the preschool staff, and parents of autistic children in the program (Bejnö et al., 2021). Their thematic analysis identified four themes—staff's competence (i.e., intervention improved staff competence for work with autistic children); autistic children's inclusion and participation (i.e., program quality information and coaching improved inclusion); collaboration (i.e., working with coaches had positive effect); and learning environment (i.e., improved as a result of APERS and coaching).

SUMMARY

The assessment of quality is a key direction for future provision of educational programs for students with autism. The findings of the studies described in this chapter demonstrate that the APERS is a reliable and valid measure of quality. It has been used to document change across time as well as difference between intervention approaches designed to improve quality. Also, the findings suggest that there are community variables, such as socioeconomic characteristics of the school, that may affect program quality. Most important, the APERS was designed for a U.S. context, and research has demonstrated that it can be adapted for a different cultural context (e.g., Sweden), and that such adaptation should occur before it is used in those contexts. In conclusion, future directions for research would be replication of the findings from these studies by other research groups, examination of the use of the APERS in a large context (e.g., scaled-up applications, replications in other countries), and a direct examination of the operating assumption that a foundation of program quality is associated with the degree to which teachers can implement evidence-based practices with high fidelity.

Frequently Asked Questions

Is there a quicker way to collect the APERS quality assessment? The APERS provides a comprehensive assessment of quality of educational programs for children and youth with autism. It is different from a rating of just classroom instruction or teacher–child interaction for which other scales can collect information in a smaller number of observations in classrooms. Educational programs for children and youth with autism extend beyond just a single classroom, in that they involve multiple students, multiple settings, and multiple individuals (e.g., teachers, related services personnel, family members). Gathering information in a single classroom for a small period of time will give an incomplete appraisal of the program.

Does quality really matter? The quality of a program is the foundation on which teachers and other service providers may implement evidence-based practices. Poor program environments are unstructured, do not have clear routines, lack clearly defined and individualized goals, do not engage in instruction that targets goals, have little cross-disciplinary collaboration, and have poor relationships with families. Such settings are not good for children and youth with autism or for the adults working in them. Implementation of evidence-based practices is nearly impossible in such settings, and the federal law does require that teachers and service providers base their instruction on research-based practices.

How can I use the assessment information? Again, the identified purpose for conducting the APERS evaluation will dictate how the information could be used. Administrators or school leaders can use the scores generated by the APERS to document the quality of the program(s) in their school district, identify training or improvement needs, and make policy decisions about future directions. For school staff, the APERS results can be used to identify strengths and challenges of the program, plan for program improvement, and even advocate to their supervisors, principals, or other school leaders for resources or program changes. As described in Chapter 4, the APERS team can generate a report that has recommendations for program improvement and may be helpful for school staff. Also, the APERS can be used to share information with parents about the quality of the program for children with autism in their school or areas in which program improvement is occurring. For that purpose, we recommend that the school staff not only show the numeric scores but also provide information about the features of the program (e.g., organized classroom, evidence-based curriculum or intervention to promote social-communication) that reflect quality.

Glossary

accepted standards for data analysis   At least 3 data points are collected before evaluating and drawing conclusions from data; level, trend, and variability are examined when inspecting data (see Item 15).

adaptive skills   Behavior necessary for independently functioning in school and community settings (e.g., going to the next class in a schedule independently, self-dressing, taking public transportation, shopping).

appropriate for student needs   Based on the developmental or functional abilities of the student. In some cases, a student may not need an accommodation because they can function independently without it. In that case, the rater may use a manual override.

assessment   Collecting information through a standard and/or systematic process about a student with autism to be used for a specific purpose (e.g., diagnosis, eligibility for services, progress monitoring). The process may be formal in standardized, norm-referenced instruments or informal (i.e., practitioner-developed data sheets, curriculum-based assessment).

behavior plan   A set of procedures (i.e., evidence-based practices; EPBs) designed to address a student's interfering behavior. This plan should be based on functional behavioral assessment (FBA) information and may be part of the student's IEP goals. Alternatively, it may be a formal plan established by the behavior support team. In either case, the plan should be specified in writing with data on the student's interfering behavior collected on a regular basis.

behavior support team   A team of professionals assembled by the school or school district to establish a formal behavioral intervention plan (BIP) to address interfering behavior.

choices   When presented with two or more alternatives, the student selects one based on their preferences.

community resource map   A list of resources in the community that students with autism may use to engage in specific skills, participate socially, or gain access to services.

consistent   Employing a practice or behavior a high percentage of the time (90%) when opportunities exist or situations call for the practice.

consultation   Professional advice about a student or classroom provided by a knowledgeable individual from outside the classroom.

expertise   Advanced knowledge or skill that conveys a high level of competency.

FBA   *see* functional behavioral assessment.

few   One or two activities, materials, or opportunities during the observation period.

fidelity   A professional's delivery of a practice or intervention as prescribed by the developer, team member, or autism team.

functional behavioral assessment (FBA)   Data collection to determine the purpose of a student's interfering behavior. FBA usually involves defining the interfering behavior, recording when it occurs, and recording events that happen directly before it (antecedent) and directly after it (consequence). The FBA may be a formal assessment designed by a school behavior support team or an evidence-based practice (EBP) used by a teacher/school staff member to plan activities in the class to address the behavior.

impressionistic observations   Observations or attributions based on an individual's personal or professional insight but not substantiated by data.

interfering behavior   Behaviors consistently displayed by the student that prevent them from engaging in learning and/or school activities. These behaviors are so problematic that they have reached a level of concern by parents, teachers, or other school staff. Examples are self-injurious behavior, aggressive behavior, elopement, and stereotypic behavior.

materials from natural environments   Items within the school, home, and community contexts included in instruction. Examples include real money when teaching money skills, textbooks from the general curriculum, and students' actual clothing when teaching dressing skills.

most   Seventy-five percent of staff, students, opportunities, and so forth. Examples include Items 2 and 7.

most team members   Seventy-five percent of the professionals and paraprofessionals directly involved in planning and implementing a student's educational program.

multiple   Three or more activities, opportunities, or materials are provided during the observation period. For example, a teacher may provide multiple opportunities for students with autism to interact with typically developing peers during the class period.

natural environment   Setting, contexts, and activities in which students without disabilities would engage.

natural reinforcer   Positive events or actions (as experienced by the student) that typically occur in normal routines or life as a consequence of a desired behavior.

peer   Any other similar-age student with or without disabilities. A more specific descriptor (e.g., typically developing) will be used if an anchor describes a specific type of peer.

peer social networks   Formation of a pattern of positive relationships among students with autism and their typically developing peers.

positive approaches   Practices designed to reduce interfering behaviors that do not include negative consequences (e.g., scolding, corporal punishment, restraint).

proactive strategies   Staff create or control a situation by causing something to happen rather than responding to it after it has happened. These strategies are often used to prevent an interfering behavior from occurring.

professional judgment   Decision by the rater based on their knowledge and expertise, the student's abilities, and the context.

prompting hierarchy   A plan for providing an increasingly more directive series of prompts (from least intrusive to most intrusive) or increasingly less direct series of prompts (from most intrusive to least intrusive) based on student's behavior.

regularly   Something is occurring or is being implemented as part of the routine and appears to occur every day (indicated by being part of the schedule or through teacher interview). For example, strategies to support transitions across settings may be regularly used.

reinforcement   Events or actions occurring after a desired behavior that are designed to increase the occurrence of the behavior in the future. Positive reinforcement is provision of a desirable event as a consequence (e.g., getting access to computer time after completing a task), and negative reinforcement is removal of an undesirable event or circumstance as a consequence (e.g., completing a low-preference or difficult task and then putting away the materials).

replacement behaviors   Student behaviors that are incompatible with or serve the same function as an identified interfering behavior; designed to increase as an interfering behavior decreases.

school staff   Individuals who come into contact with a student during the course of the student's day at school. Staff may include team members, school administrators, physical education teacher, art teacher, nurse, paraprofessionals, guidance counselors, office staff, and so on.

self-advocacy   Statement or actions by the student that positively communicate their accomplishments, requests, or desired actions or others.

self-management skills   Behaviors such as monitoring, evaluating, collecting data on, or reinforcing one's own action related to a desired behavior, or decreasing an interfering behavior.

sometimes   Activities, materials, opportunities are provided and/or are available about 25%–75% of the time.

sufficient   Enough materials are available for all students in the class or activity to participate.

task analysis   Breaking tasks into smaller and/or simpler series of steps to promote a student's learning (e.g., a complex task might be handwashing, which could begin with the steps "turn on water, pick up soap" and end with the step "dry hands on towel").

team member   School personnel directly involved in planning and/or implementing a student's educational program. These would include individuals on the IEP team (e.g., special education teacher(s), general education teachers, speech-language pathologists [SLPs]), other teachers or staff, and paraprofessionals directly supporting a student.

team members   Two or more team members, as previously defined.

References

Bejnö, H., Bölte, S., Linder, N., Långh, U., Odom, S. L., & Roll-Pettersson, L. (2021). From someone who may cause trouble to someone you can play with: Stakeholders' perspectives on preschool program quality for autistic children. *Journal of Autism and Developmental Disorders*. https://doi.org/10.1007/s10803-021-05268-2

Bejnö, H., Roll-Pettersson, L., Klintwall, L., Långh, U., Odom, S. L., & Bölte, S. (2019). Cross-cultural content validity of the Autism Program Environment Rating Scale in Sweden. *Journal of Autism and Developmental Disorders, 49*, 1853–1862.

Bejnö, H., Roll-Pettersson, L., Klintwall, L., Långh, U., Odom, S. L., & Bölte, S. (2021). Adapting the preschool environment to the needs of children on the autism spectrum in Sweden: A quasi-experimental study. *Scandinavian Journal of Occupational Therapy*. https://doi.10.1080/11038128.2021.1993330

Bhat, A. (2019). *Rating scales: Definition, survey question types, and examples.* https://www.questionpro.com/blog/rating-scale

Bronfenbrenner, U., & Morris, P. A. (2006). The bioecological model of human development. In W. Damon (Series Ed.) & R. M. Lerner (Vol. Ed.), *Handbook of child psychology: Theoretical models of human development* (pp. 793–828). Wiley.

Colorado Department of Education. (2016). *Autism program quality indicators.* Author.

Covey, S. R. (2004). *The 7 habits of highly effective people: Restoring the character ethic.* Free Press.

Crimmins, D. B., Durand, V. M., Theurer-Kaufman, K., & Everett, J. (2001). *Autism Program Quality Indicators.* New York State Education Department.

Gallagher, J. J. (2006). *Driving change in special education policy.* Paul H. Brookes Publishing Co.

Hance, M. (2020). *Considering district size when establishing your target audience* [Online article]. https://mdreducation.com/2018/04/20/school-district-sizes-target-audience

Harms, T., & Clifford, R. M. (1980). *The Early Childhood Environment Rating Scale.* Teachers College Press.

Harms, T., Clifford, R. M., & Cryer, D. (2014). *Early Childhood Environment Rating Scale, Third Edition (ECERS-3).* Teachers College Press.

Harms, T., Cryer, D., & Clifford, R. M. (2016). *Infant-toddler Environmental Rating Scale, Revised Edition.* Teachers College Press.

Harms, T., Cryer, D., Clifford, R. M., & Yazigian, N. (2022). *Family Child Care Environmental Rating Scale, Third Edition.* Teachers College Press.

Harms, T., Jacobs, E. V., & White, D. R. (2014). *School-Age Care Environment Rating Scale Updated (SACERS).* Teachers College Press.

Henson, R. K. (2001). Understanding internal consistency reliability estimates: A conceptual primer on coefficient alpha. *Measurement and Evaluation in Counseling and Development, 34*, 177–189.

Hubel, M., Hagell, P., & Sivberg, B. (2008). Brief report: Development and initial testing of a questionnaire version of the Environment Rating Scale (ERS) for assessment of residential programs for individuals with autism. *Journal of Autism and Developmental Disorders, 38*, 1178–1183. https://doi:10.1007/s10803-007-0493-y

Hume, K., Odom, S. L., Steinbrenner, J. R., Smith DaWalt, L., Hall, L. J., Kraemer, B., Tomaszewski, B., Brum, C., Szidon, K., & Bolt, D. M. (2022). Efficacy of a school-based comprehensive intervention program for adolescents with autism. *Exceptional Children, 88*(2), 223–240. https://doi.org/10.1177/00144029211062589

Hume, K., Steinbrenner, J. R., Odom, S. L., Morin, K. L., Nowell, S. W., Tomaszewski, B., Szendrey, S., McIntyre, N. S., Yücesoy-Özkan, S., & Savage, M. N. (2021). Evidence-based practices for children, youth, and young adults with autism: Third generation review. *Journal of Autism and Developmental Disorders, 51*(11), 4013–4032. https://doi.org/10.1007/s10803-020-04844-2

Individuals with Disabilities Education Improvement Act (IDEA) of 2004, PL 108-446, 20 U.S.C. §§ 1400 *et seq.*

Kahn, J., Bronte-Tinkew, J., & Theokas, C. (2008). *How can I assess the quality of my program? Tools for out-of-school time program practitioners.* Child Trends.

Kansas State Department of Education, Special Education Services. (2013). *Guide for educating students with autism spectrum disorders.* Author.

Kraemer, B. R., Odom, S. L., Tomaszewski, B., Hall, L. J., Dawalt, L., Hume, K. A., Steinbrenner, J. R., Szidon, K., & Brum, C. (2020). Quality of high school programs for students with autism spectrum disorder. *Autism: The International Journal of Research and Practice, 24*(3), 707–717. https://doi.org/10.1177/1362361319887280

Kuperminc, G. P., Seitz, S., Joseph, H., Khatib, N., Wilson, C., Collins, K., & Guecsnour, O. (2019). Enhancing program quality in a national sample of after-school settings: The role of youth-staff interactions and staff/organizational functioning. *American Journal of Community Psychology, 63*, 391–404.

LaParo, K. M., Pianta, R. C., & Stuhlman, M. (2004). The Classroom Assessment Scoring System findings from the prekindergarten year. *Elementary School Journal, 104*, 409–426.

Librera, W. L., Bryant, I., Gantwerk, B., & Tkach, B. (2004). *Autism program quality indicators: A self-review and quality improvement guide for programs serving young students with autism spectrum disorders* (PTM No. 1504.65). New Jersey Department of Education.

Maenner, M. J., Warren, Z., Williams, A. R., Amoakohene, E., Bakian, A. V., Bilder, D. A., Durkin, M. S., Fitzgerald, R. T., Furnier, S. M., Hughes, M. M., Ladd-Acosta, C. M., McArthur, D., Pas, E. T., Salinas, A., Vehorn, A., Williams, S., Esler, A., Grzybowski, A., Hall-Lande, J., . . . Shaw, K.A. (2023). Prevalence and characteristics of autism spectrum disorder among children aged 8 years—Autism and Developmental Disabilities Monitoring Network, 11 sites, United States, 2020. *MMWR Surveillance Summaries, 72*(2), 1. http://doi.org/0.15585/mmwr.ss7202a1

National Institute of Child Health and Human Development. (2006). *Study of early child care and youth development (SECCYD): Findings for children up to age 4 1/2 years* (05-4318). U.S. Government Printing Office.

Nunnally, J. C., & Bernstein, I. H. (1994). *Psychometric theory* (3rd ed.). McGraw-Hill.

Odom, S. L., Collet-Klingenberg, L., Rogers, S., & Hatton, D. (2010). Evidence-based practices for children and youth with autism spectrum disorders. *Preventing School Failure, 54*, 275–282.

Odom, S. L., Cox, A., & Brock, M. (2013). Implementation science, professional development, and autism spectrum disorders: National Professional Development Center on ASD. *Exceptional Children, 79*, 233–251.

Odom, S. L., Cox, A., Sideris, J., Hume, K. A., Hedges, S., Kucharczyk, S., Shaw, E., Boyd, B. A., Reszka, S., & Neitzel, J. (2018). Assessing quality of program environments for children and youth with autism: Autism Program Environment Rating Scale. *Journal of Autism and Developmental Disorders, 48*, 913–924.

Odom, S. L., Duda, M., Kucharczyk, S., Cox, A., & Stabel, A. (2014). Applying an implementation science framework for adoption of a comprehensive program for high school students with autism spectrum disorder. *Remedial and Special Education, 35*, 123–132.

Odom, S. L., Hall, L. J., & Suhrheinrich, J. (2020). Implementation science, behavior analysis, and supporting evidence-based practices for individuals with autism. *European Journal of Behavior Analysis, 21*(1), 55–73. https://doi:10.1080/15021149.2019.1641952

Odom, S. L., Sam, A. M., Tomaszewski, B., & Cox, A. W. (2022). Quality of educational programs for elementary school-age students with autism. *American Journal on Intellectual and Developmental Disabilities, 127*(1), 29–41. https://doi.org/10.1352/1944-7558-127.1.29

Odom, S. L., Tomaszewski, B., Perkins, Y., & Cox, A. (2021). Employing evidence-based practices for children with autism in elementary schools. *Journal of Autism and Developmental Disorders, 51*, 2308–2323. https://doi.org/10.1007/s10803-020-04706-x

Oldster, K. J. (2016). *Dead toad scrolls*. Booklocker.com.

Pirsig, R. M. (1975). *Zen and the art of motorcycle maintenance*. Bantam.

Professional Development in Autism. (n.d.). *PDA program assessment*. Experimental Education Unit, University of Washington.

Renty, J., & Roeyers, H. (2005). Students with autism spectrum disorder in special and general education schools in Flanders. *British Journal of Developmental Disabilities, 51*, 27–39. https://doi:10.1179/096979505799103795

Sam, A. M., Odom, S. L., Tomaszewski, B., Perkins, Y., & Cox, A. W. (2021). Employing evidence-based practices for children with autism in elementary schools. *Journal of Autism and Developmental Disorders, 51*(7), 2308–2323. https://doi.org/10.1007/s10803-020-04706-x

Soukakou, E. P. (2012). Measuring quality in inclusive preschool classrooms: Development and validation of the Inclusive Classroom Profile (ICP). *Early Childhood Research Quarterly, 27*, 478–488.

Soukakou, E. (2016). *Inclusive Classroom Profile*. Paul H. Brookes Publishing Co.

Soukakou, E. P., Winton, P. J., West, T. A., Sideris, J. H., & Rucker, L M. (2016). Measuring the quality of inclusive practices: Findings from the Inclusive Classroom Profile pilot. *Early Childhood Research Quarterly, 27*, 478–488.

Steinbrenner, J. R., Hume, K., Odom, S. L., Morin, K. L., Nowell, S. W., Tomaszewski, B., Szendrey, S., McIntyre, N. S., Yücesoy-Özkan, S., & Savage, M. N. (2020). *Evidence-based practices for children, youth, and young adults with autism*. University of North Carolina at Chapel Hill, Frank Porter Graham Child Development Institute, National Clearinghouse on Autism Evidence and Practice Review Team.

Suen, H. K., & Ary, D. (1989). *Analyzing quantitative behavioral observation data*. Lawrence Erlbaum Associates.

Tipton, E. (2014). How generalizable is your experiment? Comparing a sample and population through a generalizability index. *Journal of Educational and Behavioral Statistics, 39*, 478–510.

Tracy, A., Surr, W., & Richer, A. (2012). *The assessment of Afterschool Program Practices Tool (APT): Findings from the APT validation study.* National Institute on Out-of-School Time.

U.S. Department of Education, Office of Special Education and Rehabilitative Services, Office of Special Education Programs. (2022). *43rd Annual Report to Congress on the Implementation of the Individuals with Disabilities Education Act.* Author.

Van Bourgondien, M. E., Reichle, N. C., Campbell, D. G., & Mesibov, G. B. (1998). The Environmental Rating Scale (ERS): A measure of the quality of the residential environment for adults with autism. *Research in Developmental Disabilities, 19,* 381–394. https://doi:10.1016/S0891-4222(98)00012-2

Wong, C., Odom, S. L., Hume, K. A., Cox, A. W., Fettig, A., Kucharczyk, S., Brock, M. E., Plavnick, J. B., Fleury, V. P., & Schultz, T. R. (2015). Evidence-based practices for children, youth, and young adults with autism spectrum disorders: A comprehensive review. *Journal of Autism and Developmental Disorders, 49,* 1951–1966.

Yell, M. L. (2019). Endrew F. v. Douglas County School District (2017): Implications for educating students with emotional and behavioral disorders. *Behavioral Disorders, 45,* 53–62.

Index